In Memory of my dear, tender, affectionate, loving and scrupulous mother Rose Charles

To my grand- nephew Ares Aimeciel Beal Osiris

My nieces Jemima Charles, Elissa Sophie Daphnis, Sarah Michelle Daphnis, Alia Daphnis, Valencia, Youseline, Androse St Felix and Annie Charles.

Contents

Vital Steps

to a
Healthy Marriage

Martial A. Charles

PublishAmerica
Baltimore

First printing

PublishAmerica has allowed this work to remain exactly as the author intended, verbatim, without editorial input.

Hardcover 978-1-4560-9576-5
Softcover 978-1-4560-9577-2
PUBLISHED BY PUBLISHAMERICA, LLLP
www.publishamerica.com
Baltimore

Printed in the United States of America

Introduction

This book is the result of many years of observation. It is the sum total of my investigation on marriage from my childhood to the present time. As a church officer in my teenage years, I was always being invited by some couples to help them deal with many important issues in their matrimonial life. They invited me not because I was an expert in family life, but because of my family origin.

During my childhood, I thought that all couples on the four corners of the earth were happy. However, in my teenage years, I discovered that it was not so. The first time I became aware of the problems that some couples were dealing with, I was completely shocked. Since that time, I developed a profound desire to always speak about the beauty, the benefits, the significance, and the extraordinary advantages of a loving, respectful, responsible and healthy family.

Effectively, for the past two decades, God has given me the opportunity to talk about this vital issue in my preaching and seminars. The explosion of technology and the popular schools of thought in the twenty-first century seem to prevail over family values and moral principles. Therefore, we are going to go back to the root of marriage. We will investigate some crucial questions about marriage.

What is the origin of the marriage institution? Is the marriage institution a man-centered theory? Is our postmodern society better off by rejecting the moral principles of matrimonial life? Is the marriage institution outdated in the twenty-first century? Can our own choices modify God's ordinances? Can our own choices change the laws of nature? Can our own choices eliminate the laws of health? Can your own choices make another person breath for you? Can your own choices change day into night? Can your own choices change winter into summer? Are our own choices above the Moral law of God?

Because we are all free to choose what direction we want to take with our lives, does that mean that there are no consequences to our choices? Has the Judeo-Christian values lost their vitality in the twenty-first century? Do parents in the twenty-first century still have the sacred duty to raise their children morally, so that they become responsible citizens who have the fear of the Lord?

Without the institution of marriage as established by the Creator of the Cosmos, what will the future of our society be? What are the missteps to avoid in marriage? How to have a healthy marriage? How do you raise your children to be successful in this world and the world to come? How do you keep the flame of romance burning in your matrimonial life? What are the dimensions of marriage? Let's explore together these fundamental questions concerning marriage and apply the biblical guidelines in our matrimonial life for our own welfare and happiness.

Martial Aimeciel Charles

Chapter 1
The Origin Of Marriage

A virtuous Christian woman is like an inexhaustible fountain that provides purified water, honey and all kinds of delicious fruits no matter what the circumstances.

Martial A. Charles

Living in an era where biblical principles and family values are regarded by some people as burdens to satisfy their sinful desires and passions, all kinds of unhealthy opinions and promotions are emerging regarding the sacredness of the institution of marriage. Human beings are so blinded by sin that some of them pretend that the absolute Moral Law of the Maker of heaven and earth, the biblical ordinances and the vital family principles, constitute a threat to their freedom and their independence in living according to their sinful nature. From the first week of the creation of the world for the human race, the Creator of the universe clearly defined marriage without any ambiguity

Unfortunately, in order to please self, some of the sinful mortal beings of our generation have redefined marriage according to their feelings and their own sinful concepts. It is a big mistake for people to make choices for their own lives according to the popular erroneous views of our society. God created us with the mental faculty to think healthily, and to analyze things and to come to the right decision for our own welfare. Once a person makes a choice, it is his or her choice. He or she cannot blame another person for the choice that has been made. You are responsible for your choices. Therefore, think healthily, honestly and responsibly.

Have you ever asked yourself: Where does marriage come from? Have you ever asked yourself: What is the main purpose of marriage? Have you ever taken the time to ask yourself: Why did God create mankind in His image? Have you ever asked yourself: What is the fundamental element of the relational aspect of God's image in mankind? Have you ever asked yourself: Is there a parallel between the Godhead and marriage? Have you ever asked yourself: What is the most basic and significant social relationship to mankind?

Have you ever asked yourself: Could we have a healthy society without the institution of marriage as God had established it? Have you ever asked yourself: What is God's design for marital relationship? Have you ever asked yourself: Why the imagery of marriage in the New Testament is used to describe the relationship between Jesus Christ and His church? Have you ever asked yourself: Is the indissoluble marriage union man's work or God's Work? Do you know that monogamous, heterosexual marriage is God's Norm for humankind?

We are living in an imperfect world. I am persuaded that we are all aware of that. However, the Maker of heaven and earth is still in the process of guiding the human race in the right direction by all kinds of visible and invisible means. There are all kinds of associations, professions, institutions, organizations and establishments all over the world; they all have their importance and reason for being. All of them have an origin and a founder. Above all, there is a specific purpose for each of them.

Each of these institutions has its requirements, procedures and policies. To join and to work for these organizations, one must respect and follow their rules and their guiding principles. Furthermore, before getting hired by any of these institutions, you must sign an agreement affirming that you will follow and respect the core values of the said institution. Of course, we don't have any problem with that. Our focus is going to be specifically on the institution of marriage. However, I must tell you that there are human institutions and divine institutions.

There is an enormous difference between a human institution and a divine institution. Marriage is a divine institution. No creature both either in the natural or the supernatural realms has the moral authority to change this sacred institution. No sinful being could modify it to satisfy his or her desires and passions. Any sinful being can choose to live as he or she wants without any regard for the core values of the marriage institution. Nevertheless, his or her choices cannot and will never be able to modify the guiding principles of the marriage institution.

The Supreme Ruler of the cosmos is the Founder of the institution of marriage. The purpose of this vital institution surpasses human reasoning, understanding, intellect, desire and choice. Therefore, I am convinced that you are ready to investigate with me the origin of marriage. I pray that God will open your intellect to grasp the vital significance of this crucial issue in the twenty-first century.

Contrary to the popular views of naturalism and secularism in the twenty-first century, on the sixth day of the creation week, the Creator of heaven and earth established the institution of marriage for the eternal happiness and the well-being of the human race. As the Supreme Loving Father of mankind, God had prepared everything before He created man. When God decided to create Adam and Eve, they had everything at their disposal.

According to the biblical account, everything was perfect. "And the LORD God said, "It is not good that man should be alone; I will make him a helper comparable to him" (Genesis 2:18). Before creating and giving Eve to Adam, God chose to create the animals and the birds. He granted to Adam the privilege of giving names to all the birds and the animals. Yes, Adam was the one who gave names to all the birds and the animals on planet earth (Genesis 2: 19). They were all male and female.

God created the birds and every living creature according to their kind (Genesis 1: 2). Adam was the only one who was alone. "So the LORD God caused the man to fall into a deep sleep; and while he was sleeping, he took one of the man's ribs and closed up the place with flesh. Then the LORD God made a woman from the rib he had taken out of the man, and he brought her to the man. The man said, "This is now bone of my bones and flesh of my flesh; she shall be called woman, for she was taken out of man. Therefore a man shall leave his father and mother and be joined to his wife, and they shall become one flesh" (Genesis 2: 21-24).

When Adam met Eve for the first time, he was very happy. I am unable to give you a complete description of the first loving meeting of Adam and Eve. However, I am going to give you an idea of the excitement of Adam. When Adam saw Eve for the first time, he was really excited.

Yes, Adam was overjoyed to see Eve.

Yes, Adam was delighted to see Eve.

Yes, Adam was enchanted to see Eve.

Yes, Adam was thrilled to see Eve.

Yes, Adam was elated to see Eve.

Yes, Adam was animated to see Eve.

Yes, Adam was energized to see Eve.

Yes, Adam was charmed to see Eve.

Yes, Adam was captivated to see Eve.

Yes, Adam was enthralled to see Eve.

Yes, Adam was enamored to see Eve.

Yes, Adam was fascinated to see Eve.

Yes, Adam was mesmerized to see Eve.

Yes, Adam was contented to see Eve.

Yes, Adam was tickled to see Eve.

Yes, Adam was exhilarated to see Eve.

Yes, Adam was pleased to see Eve.

Yes, Adam was relieved to see Eve.

Yes, Adam was ecstatic to see Eve.

Yes, Adam was jubilant to see Eve.

Yes, Adam was euphoric to see Eve.

Yes, Adam was on cloud nine to see Eve.

Yes, Adam was in seventh heaven to see Eve.

Absolutely, Adam was totally in love with Eve. Adam was delighted to find his incomparable helper. Unquestionably, Adam was elated to see his sweetheart, darling, honey, sugar, baby, sweetie and dearest Eve. Eve was so beautiful, charming, attractive and pure in all aspects of her life that she elevated Adam's emotional temperature to 100 degrees. Adam was so delighted to see Eve that he charmed her with the following breathtaking poetic affirmation:

"This is now bone of my bones

And flesh of my flesh;

She shall be called woman,

Because she was taken out of man" (Genesis 2: 23).

Absolutely, Adam was the first poet on planet earth. I imagine that Eve was speechless. She took her time to contemplate and admire her prince charming, the poet Adam. The Supreme Sovereign of the universe created Adam and Eve perfect and mature physically, mentally, emotionally and spiritually. Both Adam and Eve were covered with the glory of God. It was a magnificent atmosphere of love, joy, obedience, mutual respect, peace, perfect communication, peace of mind and exhilaration on all levels.

God Himself celebrated the first marriage on planet earth in the Garden of Eden. "God bless them; and God said to them, " Be fruitful and multiply, and fill the earth, and subdue it; and rule over the fish of the sea and over the birds of the sky and over every living thing that moves on the earth" (Genesis 1: 28).

Ellen G. White asserted: "God celebrated the first marriage. Thus the institution has for its originator the Creator of the universe. "Marriage is honourable"; it was one of the first gifts of God to man, and it is one of the two institutions that, after the fall, Adam brought with him beyond the gates of Paradise. When the divine principles are recognized and obeyed in this relation, marriage is a blessing; it guards the purity and happiness of the race, it provides for man's social needs, it elevates the physical, the intellectual, and the moral nature."

God has played seven fundamental roles in the union of Adam and Eve. He was the Creator, the Father, the Matchmaker, the Counselor, the Provider, the Preacher and the blessing Giver of the first nuptial ceremony on planet earth. The wedding of Adam and Eve took place on the sixth day of the creation week, meaning on Friday. So, the marriage was the first indissoluble institution that the Almighty King of the cosmos established on the first week of creation on planet earth. On the seventh day of the creation week, God established the second indissoluble institution, which is the Sabbath (Gen 2: 1-3).

The Maker of heaven and earth founded these two unbreakable institutions for the happiness and the well-being of the human race. Now, we know the Preacher and the day on which the wedding of Adam and Eve took place. But, there are other important questions that we don't discuss yet. For example: Who were the guests at the wedding of Adam and Eve? Who were the singers and the musicians? What was the menu? How were Adam and Eve dressed for their wedding? And, where did Adam go with Eve for their honeymoon?

Adam and Eve got married during the most glorious and magnificent week on planet earth. They had the privilege of enjoying not only the glory of creation, but also and above all else, the glory of the Supreme Lawgiver of the cosmos. From Job 38: 7, I deduce that the singers, the musicians and the guests in Adam's wedding were the heavenly angels and the ambassadors of the other planets. Definitely, the heavenly hosts were present. Humanly speaking, it is impossible for me to find the right expression to describe the solemnity of that ceremony. What an incomparable privilege to see face to face the angelical choir praising the Creator-King!

The Bible gives us the description of the menu at Adam's wedding. "And God said, Behold, I have given you every herb yielding seed, which is upon the face of all the earth, and every tree, in which is the fruit of a tree yielding seed; to you it shall be for food" (Genesis 1: 29). Therefore, the menu at Adam's wedding was a vegetarian menu. This is the original menu that God gave to the human race to live healthily. God allowed man to eat meat after the flood (Gen 9: 3). But God did not say to eat all kinds of meats. He makes a clear difference between clean and unclean food (Leviticus 11). So, for your own health, it is completely better to follow God's instruction regarding the original menu.

I am convinced that a lot of women are very curious about Eve's wedding dress. The question concerning Eve's wedding dress is very important for women. It reminds them of their own wedding dress. However, don't forget that our concept of physical dress comes from our sinful world and our sinful nature. For Adam and Eve, it was completely different. They were created in the image of God in a perfect world. There was no sin at that time. So, for their wedding, Adam and Eve were dressed or covered with the holiness, knowledge, glory, character and the perfection of God. Adam and Eve didn't have on any physical dress (Genesis 2: 25). They were in complete purity and moral innocence.

As the pinnacle of God's creative work, Adam was delighted to have on his side the first and the most beautiful woman on earth; and to receive power, authority, dominion and honor from his Creator over the other earthly creatures. Effectively, God placed Adam as the ruler of planet earth. What an extraordinary opportunity! Adam and Eve were celebrating the luxury of divine benediction in its fullness. The last question is about Adam's honeymoon. Adam and Eve didn't travel to another planet for their honeymoon. "The LORD God planted a garden eastward in Eden, and there He put the man whom He had formed" (Genesis 2: 8).

There was no need for Adam and Eve to travel in another planet for their honeymoon. God had prepared a beautiful place for them to joyfully enjoy their union and to live happily. And also, they had the privilege of being in the presence of God. I think that Adam was very thankful to God for Eve. I assume that Adam praised God in a special way before starting the exploration of Eve's universe. I also imagine that Adam exposed his poetic skills to Eve in a deeper level during their honeymoon. If in our sinful world, honeymoon is so sweet; I wonder how it was for Adam and Eve. Always remember to praise God not only for your honeymoon, but every time that you are drinking the pure nectar of your juice, which is your wife.

Marriage is a divine institution. Marriage is and remains forever the interminable blending between a man and a woman. This is God's plan for the welfare of the human race.

According to God's plan for the happiness of the human race, man should not stay under the caring protection of his parents forever. At the appropriate time, man should leave his parents and establish a new family component with his wife. For Adam, it was different because he was born mature in all aspects of life. So, God gave him his wife right away.

There is a key point that I don't want you to miss. Our loving heavenly Father didn't give to Adam two wives or anything else. During the creation week, our Creator was very clear about the establishment and the indestructibility of the first institution, which is marriage. In spite of our sinful nature, God created us with enough intelligence to understand His instruction through the power of the Holy Spirit. You don't have to be a Bible scholar to discover the intention of God for husband and wife in Genesis 2: 24. It reads: "For this reason a man shall leave his father and his mother, and be joined to his wife; and they shall become one flesh".

God's intention for husband and wife was, has been, is and will always be monogamy. God didn't give two or three wives to Adam. God instituted marriage on the sixth day of creation. Marriage is and remains forever the unending joining together of a man and a woman. Adam had sex with Eve during the first day of their honeymoon, not before they got married. Both of them were virgins. Adam and Eve were pure and innocent physically, morally, emotionally, mentally and spiritually. We are living in a sinful world. There are all kinds of theories about marriage. We are all free to use our free will as we wish.

But, we should always remember that our choices do not, cannot and will never be able to amend God's Constitution for the human race. God's way was, has been, is and will always be the best way. If we violate human laws at any level, we will pay the consequences. If we violate natural laws, definitely, we will pay the consequences. If we violate health laws, there is no doubt about it, we will surely pay the consequences. Why do so many people in this world think that they can violate God's

Moral Law to satisfy their passions and selfish desires without expecting that the consequences will absolutely come?

Marriage is not a man-centered theory. It is a divine institution. It transcends human power, concepts, choices, opinions and desires. We are living in an imperfect and sinful world. There is no doubt about it; we are all free to do whatever we want with our lives. At the same time, we must always remember that our choices cannot change and determine God's intended way of life for the human race. Life is a gift from the Almighty God of the universe to mankind. We are all accountable to God for the way that we choose to live.

One day, every single human being on planet earth will have to give account to God for his or her life. The intention of God in giving the gift of life to the human race was to produce delicious fruits and all good things for the happiness of mankind. Some of the fruits are the following:

Love

Obedience

Compliance

Submission

Adoration

Worship

Praise

Total surrender to God

Allegiance to the Maker of heaven and earth

Giving yourself lovingly to the Creator of the cosmos

Being devoted to live by God's guidance

Conformity

Duty

Purity

Integrity

Honesty
Loyalty
Morality
Decency
Modesty
Unity
Sincerity
Harmony
Fidelity
Peace
Justice
Joy
Respect
Frankness
Goodness
Kindness
Fairness
Gentleness
Faithfulness
Bluntness
Uprightness
Truthfulness
Forthrightness
Righteousness
Trustworthiness
Godliness
Saintliness
Holiness.

What do you choose to do with your life? Do you choose to produce fruits for the glory of God? Or, do you choose to satisfy your own desires and passions? Of course, everyone is free to make his or her own choices. Our choices determine our direction in life and shape our future. Remember that the first couple on planet earth was Adam and Eve. As the Supreme Monarch of the cosmos established it in the Garden of Eden, marriage is and remains forever the unbreakable union between a man and a woman.

God's perfect plan for the human race is the unity of a man and a woman in holy matrimony. This plan was not meant for a few generations, but for all generations. No human alternative, design, structure, plan, amendment, referendum, vote, choice or decree will ever be able to replace it. As God designed it on the sixth day of creation, the guiding principles of the institution of marriage are and remain forever and ever the best way for the welfare and the true happiness of mankind.

Chapter 2
Marriage Preparation

An honest Christian man reflects God's character not only in his matrimonial life, but also in his life in general through the guidance of the Holy Spirit.

Martial A. Charles

Anyone who aspires to be a lawyer, a medical doctor, a scientist, an astronaut, an engineer, a theologian, a professor or a psychologist must have a meticulous preparation. You have to climb the different steps in the educational ladder to reach your goal. You must be willing to go from Kindergaden to Graduate School. After your graduation from graduate school, you have to be officially licensed to practice your profession as a medical doctor or a psychologist. So, it is not something that you can take lightly. Without the required preparation, you won't be allowed to practice as a lawyer; this applies to many other professions.

However, it is completely different for marriage. In spite of the vital importance of marriage for the human race, you don't have to spend eighteen to twenty years in school. And, you don't have to pass any final exam to get married. Therefore, how and where are we to get the necessary training to have a successful marriage? Does the world concept of marriage substitutes God's original plan for mankind?

Adam received his matrimonial training from God. Therefore, the parents have the responsibility to begin training their children at home. "And these words which I command you today shall be in your heart. You shall teach them diligently to your children, and shall talk of them when you sit in your house, when you walk by the way, when you lie down, and when you rise up. You shall bind them as a sign on your hand, and they shall be as frontlets between your eyes. You shall write them on the doorposts of your house and on your gates" (Deuteronomy 6: 6-9).

It is the responsibility of the parents to teach the moral principles of God to their children. Parents should teach their children by their examples. Believe it or not, the way that parents treat each other has a lasting impact on their children. The type of conjugal environment that the children grow up will be recorded in their memory for the rest of their lives. So, parents should do their best through the guidance of the Holy Spirit to establish an atmosphere of love, mutual respect, responsibility, peace, integrity, honesty, obedience, collaboration, communication and spiritual growth.

Addressing his spiritual son Timothy, the apostle Paul declared: "You have been taught the Holy Scriptures from childhood, and they have given you the wisdom to receive the salvation that comes by trusting in Christ Jesus" (2 Timothy 3:15). At home, from Timothy's infancy, his mother and his grandmother taught him the moral principles and the fear of God. All parents have a sacred duty to begin the formation of the character of their children from their early days according to the word of God.

I am very thankful to my parents. From my childhood, my parents taught me a lot of things that I will apply for the rest of my life. From my infancy, my parents taught me honesty, mutual respect, loyalty, integrity, morality, modesty, decency, obedience to parents, obedience to God, obedience to authority and discipline. I had also the privilege of having my grandmother who was a great role model for me. There are a lot of basic things that are very important in life. Even though there was a maid and other people who were in charge of housekeeping in my home, my mother made it a requirement for me to clean my room, to make my bed and participate in the household activities.

My loving mother taught me how to cook and how to iron my clothes. She did the same thing for my brothers and my sister. The rules of the house were very clear. There was a time to pray, a time to go to bed, a time to study, a time to do our homework, a time to play, a time for family discussion, a time to eat, a time to participate in housekeeping and so forth. My parents didn't only teach us by their words how to treat and respect each other and other people, but they also taught us by their actions. They taught me the sacredness of marriage. They placed in my mind a mental picture of a healthy marriage. My grandmother used to describe the happy conjugal life of my great grandparents over and over again.

Of course, when we become adults, we have our own experiences in life. We make our own choices. And also, we learn a lot of things in our academic preparation. However, what we have learned in our childhood plays an important role in our concepts and perceptions of marriage. Children who grow up in a healthy family, have more ammunition to resist against peer pressure, low self-esteem, unhealthy habits, and the desire to follow the wrong crowd. They are more stable psychologically and emotionally.

On the other hand, children who grow up in an unhealthy family have an empty hole in their lives. It is easier for them to follow the wrong crowd looking for love, guidance and acceptance. Some of them may fill this empty hole positively.

But, most of them will fill it negatively by choosing the wrong path of life. It will manifest even in their adult lives. For example, a girl who grew up in a family where her parents were involved in fighting and cheating, the scene is recorded in her mind. It is like a tape recorder. You record something and you press the pause button. Be aware that the pause button doesn't erase the message.

Therefore, whenever you press the play button, you will hear the message that you have recorded. If the girl never gets any professional help in that matter, it will manifest in her conjugal life. When she gets married, it could be many years later; she will be very suspicious and susceptible toward her husband without showing it visibly. Internally, she is fighting a big fight. Even if she knows that her husband is faithful, her insecurity is troubling her. Time after time, her negative experience with her parents in her childhood will come and go in her mind. She will develop a lot of negative imaginations. She could choose to live in denial by acting like everything is fine with her. Or, she could choose to be honest with herself by lovingly addressing her trouble with her husband in order that she can find some help to live peacefully.

She has to learn how to trust her partner to live peacefully and healthily. It is completely better for her to seek help instead of living in denial. If she doesn't seek any help, sooner or later, she will have some unintelligent reactions toward her husband that will prove that there is something wrong with her. And also, she could choose to practice the same things in her matrimonial life. Unfortunately, she could be very cleaver in practicing those destructive habits.

Seeking help to live in peace is not a sign of weakness. On the contrary, it is a sign of wisdom. It is the same thing for a boy who grew up in a dysfunctional family. If disrespect, verbal abuse, emotional abuse, physical abuse and cheating were the lot of his childhood surroundings, he could choose to repeat them in his conjugal life. If he doesn't get any help to deal with these issues, when he gets married, it is going to be very difficult for him to trust his wife and treat her respectfully. When there is an empty hole in the life of a child, sooner or later in his teenage years, he or she will find a way to fill it. Most of the times, children will fill it negatively and destructively if they don't have a mentor.

There are many ways that they could fill it. They could do so by embracing promiscuity, using destructive substances, smoking, drinking, following the wrong crowd and many other harmful habits. The children who grow up in a healthy family are not perfect. They also have a sinful nature just as the other children who grow up in a dysfunctional family. They have the ability and they could make wrong choices at any time. However, the big difference is the healthy training that they receive from their infancy will guide them in the right path of life. So, parents have a great responsibility to create a loving environment for their children, one that is based on love, respect, morality and all the other biblical principles.

Parents are not responsible for the choices of their children in their adulthood. However, they are responsible for the environment of their children's childhood. King Solomon said: "Train up a child in the way he should go, even when he is old he will not depart from it" (Proverbs 22: 6). The best way to train a child is according to the Wisdom of God. The wisdom of this world will lead your child to the wrong path. If you train your child in smoking, drinking alcohol, promiscuity, hateful speeches, lies, dishonesty, racism, selfishness and disrespect for God and authority, you will literally lead your child to the path of self-destruction.

Talking about Abraham, God declared: "For I have chosen him so that he will direct his children and his household after him to keep the way of the LORD by doing what is right and just, so that the LORD will bring about for Abraham what He has promised him"(Genesis 18: 19). Do you train your children to keep the way of the Lord by doing what is right and just?

There is a group of people who chooses not to get married. There are others who are deeply afraid of marriage. Many of them are great professionals. For some of them, the reason is due to a destructive experience that they had in their childhood with their parents. In their infancy, they saw their parents fighting, beating and disrespecting each other. So, they made up their mind that they would not get married. They believe that their own experience will be the same. Some women are afraid of men who look like their father. Whenever they see a man that has the appearance of their father, they remember their childhood nightmare. Most of them do not seek professional help regarding their traumatic childhood experiences.

To avoid thinking about marriage, some of them choose to focus on a specific career. They completely devote themselves to their career. And, they are very successful. They always act like they are completely fine. But, their childhood shock is still there. It would be wiser for them to see a Christian professional counselor. Even if they are very successful in their career, their childhood wounds are not healed. The only way to find the correct balance to their lives is to deal healthily with their childhood emotional wounds. Definitely, they should seek professional help for their own welfare. In that situation, it is a wining strategy and a must to see a Christian professional counselor.

Internally, they are still suffering. Instead of seeking professional help to heal the nightmare of their infancy, some of them prefer to live in promiscuity by transgressing the Moral Law of God. The problem is not in the institution of marriage itself. The problem is in the family they grew up in. Unfortunately, their parents did not establish a healthy environment during their childhood. Rebelling against the institution of marriage will not solve the problem. On the contrary, it creates more problems.

There is nothing wrong with the institution of marriage. Marriage is sacred. But, their traumatic childhood nightmare was very bad. That doesn't mean that they cannot have a healthy marriage. That doesn't mean that their own marriage is going to be the same as their childhood nightmare. The first step is to see a professional Christian counselor. The second step is to pray and ask God to give you a loving, honest, respectful and responsible Christian spouse to enjoy your life morally, peacefully and healthily.

The Christian life is wonderful. God's way will always be the best way. God didn't create us to live in promiscuity and all the other licentious modes of this world. God created us to be married as male and female. According to God's plan for the human race, a man and a woman should live together as husband and wife, not as boyfriend and girlfriend. By choosing to live away from God's original plan, they create more troubles in their own lives. God loves you dearly. He is waiting for you to make peace with Him in order that you can enjoy fully your inner peace. True inner peace is found only in God. Human reasoning, money, power, fame, celebrity and all the popular modes and teachings of our era cannot and will never be able to produce it.

There are other people who choose not to get married. Some of them are afraid of marriage because they have been in a painful and horrible relationship. Internally, they are cultivating some fear, anger and hostility feelings. However, they will not show it visibly. They concentrate themselves fully on their career. They may always present themselves as joyous and happy. Their determination will help them to greatly succeed in their career. Some of them will become famous. They might climb the last step in the human ladder of success. A lot of people around the world would consider them as the happiest persons on earth because of their wealth, popularity, fame and world influence.

Nonetheless, their emotional wound is still troubling their

lives. They might practice all kinds of unhealthy habits to put their internal wound on pause. However, the true healing will only come when they decide to deal with their negative experience honestly by making peace with God in their inner soul and seeking help from a professional Christian counselor. Then, they will realize that they are responsible for their heartbreaking experience that comes from their unhealthy habits. It is the result of their own choices. They will take full responsibility for their mistake and move forward healthily with their lives, never to repeat the same gaffe through the guidance of the Holy Spirit.

Choosing to revolt against the institution of marriage cannot and will never be able to heal their pain. On the contrary, it creates more troubles in their lives. For their own peace of mind, it would be wiser for them to choose to follow the way of our Creator. When we make the choice to follow God's way in every aspect of our life, we protect and preserve ourselves from many horrifying and hurtful experiences in life. Marriage preparation starts at home. The formation of character of all the great men and women in the world began at home.

All parents on the entire globe should train their children from their childhood according to the way of the Most High God. It is the sacred duty of parents to train their children from childhood to be successful in this world and to be ready for the glorious second coming of our Lord and Savior Jesus Christ to establish His eternal Kingdom of love and peace for all.

The parents who train their children according to the word of God guide them on how to make the choice to live under the influence of the Holy Spirit instead of according to our own their sinful nature. Without that preparation, the children will always act according to their passions and selfish desires. The parents are responsible for training their children from infancy according to the word of God how to be successful in all aspects of their lives.

From my childhood, my parents taught me the moral principles of life. My father was my childhood hero. My dear and beloved mother formed my character. My father taught me self-control, discipline, healthy thinking, how to focus on my dream until its realization. My beloved grandmother taught me wisdom, discernment and contentment. Whenever I went to see my grandmother, she always taught me something positive. I enjoyed spending time at my grandmother's house.

When I was a teenager, my grandmother gave me a parable. She said: "Whenever you leave your parents' house to visit a different place, when you get to that place, if you see that everybody is dancing on two feet; you, always remember to dance on one foot." I did not understand the parable. So, I asked my grandmother: "What does that mean? " Effectively, she explained the parable to me.

My grandmother told me: "Your father and your mother taught you the moral principles from your childhood. Now, you have become a teenager. Remember not to follow the wrong crowd. Wherever you are and whatever the decision that you will have to make in life, you should always remember to make your decision in accordance with the principles that you have learned from your childhood. I greatly assure you, if you apply them in your life, you will have a peaceful, prosperous and blessed life." By God's grace, I can testify that my grandmother was completely right.

In our family discussion, my father always used an illustration to teach us the realities of life. My parents created an environment where we were free to express ourselves. In his teenage years, my older brother met a beautiful girl. She was so beautiful that my brother was willing to give up everything to marry her. My father saw the obsession of my brother. So, he called a family meeting. My father gave a wonderful illustration to show us that our education should be our focus. We will always have time to find a partner in life. However, if we neglect our education in our teenage years, we could put ourselves in a difficult position to prevent us from having a bright future.

My father declared: "Let's say that I take you all out to visit a flower garden. When we get to our destination, there is a big a gate at the entrance of the garden. While we are waiting for the gate-keeper to open the gate, we take a look inside; we see that there are only beautiful flowers in the entire garden. When we get inside, if I ask you to choose a flower, what method would you use to pick your flower?" We all gave our opinion. At the end, we had adopted my older brother's suggestion by stating that we would choose the most beautiful one. We had all missed the essential point. My father affirmed: "All the flowers do not have the same odor. The most important point is to smell them and choose the one that has the best odor." He continued by saying: "When you are looking for a partner, beauty should not be your number one priority. You should look first for virtue, spirituality, quality, goodness, moral character and family of origin." Effectively, my father was on the right track. The friendship lasted only for a few weeks. I have learned that lesson from my childhood.

Marriage is a lifetime commitment. Marriage preparation has many phases. Even if we receive the first lessons of marriage at home, we should continue to learn new skills and new methods. There are many ways to keep the process of learning alive. We can buy books about marriage. There are always marriage seminars offered in different places. We should do our best to participate. We could take some courses on family life. We could watch family programs on television. We could also listen to family programs on the radio. We should do our best to see a Christian professional marriage counselor. We should read and meditate on the marvelous instructions regarding marriage in the Bible. Above all else, we should always pray and ask God for His guidance.

Chapter 3
Mistakes To Avoid In Marriage

A dishonest, irresponsible and unfaithful woman could make you believe not by faith, but visibly that an orange tree produces grapes regularly in each season.

Martial A. Charles

There are different types of contracts. Whenever you choose to sign a contract, you know for sure that you are bound to the conditions within the contract. Before putting your signature to the contract, you are fully aware of the consequences and penalties if you choose to breach the contract. So, you make the choice to sign or not to sign the contract. Therefore, a contract is not something that you have to take lightly. It is your responsibility to respect the conditions within the contract. It could take few years or few months to prepare for a wedding ceremony. The wedding ceremony is only for one or few days.

However, marriage is for life. We are all human beings. All human beings make mistakes. But, when we know that something is wrong, we have the responsibility to avoid it and stay away from it. If we choose to move forward anyway, we should also remember that sooner or later the consequences will follow our choices.

The first example is in the Bible. Eve knew very well that she should be near Adam. She was attracted by something else. She deliberately made her own choice to follow her feelings instead of the principles of matrimonial life. She voluntarily left Adam to go in a different place that made her fell good about her own desires. She was fully aware of the divine instruction. However, she decided to satisfy her own feelings. She knew very well that what she was doing was wrong. That's why she didn't consult her husband about her adventure. In her adventure away from her husband, she was flirting with the devil through the serpent without realizing it. And, you know the result including the consequences of her destructive mistakes.

So the first destructive mistake to avoid in marriage is to stop flirting with your ex boyfriend, girlfriend, co-worker, or anybody else. As soon as you make the decision to get married, it doesn't matter how long you have been with your ex or what experience you have had with him or her, there must be a border between you and him or her. If you don't take your marriage seriously, sooner or later, devastation, desolation, humiliation, scandal, painful outcomes and many more negative things will visit you and live with you for a long period of time.

It is your responsibility to secure that border by any means. No one else will secure it for you. When you get married, it is a destructive mistake to spend your time discussing your sexual life with your ex instead of with your spouse. There is a big difference between a spouse and a former boyfriend or girlfriend. Your spouse is your partner for life. Your sexual life is your business with your partner. A lot of people do not understand the power of words. Definitely, your constant sexual conversation with your ex will surely produce its fruit. When you put yourself in that situation, you are practicing mental adultery.

If you don't stop it, at the appropriate time, you will see its completion. If you really want to save your marriage and enjoy life healthily with your spouse, stop breaking the different facets of marriage boundaries to please your sinful nature. For your own happiness and the happiness of your entire family, develop a sincere, loving, respectful and honest relationship with your spouse.

There are some people who think that they are smart by lying and living in ruse and denial in their matrimonial life. Instead of taking full responsibility for their selfish and destructive behaviors and getting rid of them, some of them let their spouse know that he or she, the ex, is just a friend.

I have known a few couples who were in that terrible situation. And also, I have seen the detrimental results. There was a couple that was facing this dilemma. The husband was a well-educated man; his wife was closer to her ex- boyfriend than him. When he knew about it, he politely discussed the issue with her. Unfortunately, she didn't care at all about his concern. According to the husband 's testimony, she said to him:" He was my friend before I met you."

In other word, she told him that she would keep her so-called friendship with her ex- boyfriend anyway. The husband was a quiet guy. Regrettably, there are some women who think that a quiet man is someone that they can easily play as they wish. Maybe, they develop this concept from the environment they grew up in.

However, what they don't think about is that a quiet man can be very analytical. Even if he doesn't say anything, he is observing everything. He might not jump to a conclusion right away, but he is firm in his decision. This particular wife treated her husband as a third class citizen and as the guardian of her yard. She was proud to disrespect her husband, claiming: "This is the way that man deserved to be treated." On the contrary, she treated her ex boyfriend respectfully as she would a king. By destroying her own life, she thought that she was very smart. A few years later, her relationship with her ex boyfriend crossed the red line. The quiet husband quietly told her: "Good bye."

Marriage is not a game. It is not something that you should take lightly. Believe it or not, you will be accountable to God for the way that you choose to live your conjugal life. You may not think about it during your self-deception adventure. There is no doubt about it, whenever you decide to break the boundaries of your marriage to satisfy the passions and unsanctified desires of your sinful nature, you will have to deal with the destructive effects of your own choice for the rest of your life.

When you get married, after Jesus Christ, your spouse should be the most important person in your life. You should prove it by your deeds and your words.

When you choose to get married, there are limits that must always be respected.

- You must respect God.
- You must respect yourself.
- You must respect your spouse.
- You must respect the boundaries in marriage.
- You must respect your commitment to your partner.
- You must respect your commitment to be faithful to each other.
- When you get married, you take a vow with your spouse.
- Not with your ex- boyfriend/girlfriend or anybody else.
- When you get married, you must do your best to always live honestly with your spouse.
- When you get married, you are condemned to cherish your partner.

- When you get married, you are condemned to be faithful to your spouse.
- When you get married, you are condemned to have one life with your partner.
- When you get married, you are condemned to be attached emotionally to your spouse.
- When you get married, you are condemned to fully reject the double life philosophy.
- When you get married, you are condemned to share your deepest intimacy only with your partner.
- When you get married, you are condemned to be closer to your spouse.
- When you get married, you are condemned to break up with selfishness.
- When you get married, you are condemned to spend significant time with your partner.
- When you get married, you are responsible to develop a healthy relationship with your partner.

When you get married, you are condemned to eliminate completely the following elements in your life:

Lie

Ruse

Trick

Malice

Deceitful intent

Manipulation

Denial

Resentment

Dishonesty

Self-importance

Untrustworthiness

Fake appearance

Secret relationship

Superiority complex

Infidelity

Animosity and disrespectful attitude.

When you get married, you are condemned before God to work together with your spouse in everything to establish in your conjugal life an atmosphere based on the following ingredients:

1. Love
2. Honesty
3. Integrity
4. Morality
5. Amiability
6. Affability
7. Decency
8. Courtesy
9. Cordiality
10. Joviality
11. Collaboration
12. Completion,
13. Devotion
14. Sanctification
15. Affection
16. Attention
17. Recognition
18. Appreciation

19. Understanding
20. Sharing
21. Caring,
22. Supporting
23. Complimenting
24. Encouraging
25. Helping,
26. Congratulating
27. Singing the glory of God
28. Praising the Maker of heaven and earth
29. Worshipping the Creator of the Cosmos
30. Tenderness
31. Sacred caress
32. Kindness
33. Holiness
34. Friendliness
35. Openness
36. Receptiveness
37. Responsiveness
38. Gentleness
39. Peacefulness
40. Kindheartedness and helpfulness.

The destructive mistakes to avoid in marriage are:
Flirting with your ex, co-worker or anybody else.
Cultivating acrimony and rancor toward your spouse.
Treating your partner as a second-class citizen.
Developing your deepest emotional bond for someone

other than your partner.

Putting yourself voluntarily in dangerous territory.

Disregarding your spouse's concerns.

Disregarding God's instruction about marriage.

Putting self, feelings and lust above the biblical principles of marriage.

Feeding your mind with licentious passions and deceitfulness.

Living a double life.

Using, abuse and misuse your partner's goodness.

Putting your spouse down for your ex or anybody else.

Humiliating your partner publicly.

Giving yourself to your partner partially and hypocritically.

Crossing the boundaries in marriage whenever you wish.

Living and acting selfishly with your partner.

Having secret intimate relationships.

Disrespecting your partner as you wish.

Physical abuse.

Verbal abuse.

Emotional and psychological abuses.

Name- calling

Violent behavior and tyrannical attitudes.

Spending your time cheating and flirting on social networks with the so-called "online friends."

Ignoring your spouse's input

Taking your marriage for granted and not spending significant time with your partner.

The other destructive mistakes to avoid in marriage are:

Letting the in-laws control your marriage.

Giving the control of your marriage to your friends.

Quarrelsome behavior

Lying pattern

Dishonesty

Unreliability

Disrespect and a bitter-tongue

Misleading appearance

An Uncontrolled tongue

Carelessness

Impertinent attitude

Living in deception, lying and refutation.

During the courtship, some people choose to present themselves as angels. It is a premeditate game to get married. They choose to lie about everything just to reach their goal. They act in a certain way to show that they are the holiest persons on earth. After the wedding, they congratulate themselves for fabricating, playing and winning their game with their partner. They consider themselves very clever. However, they concentrate only on one angle. Their focus is only on what they want to accomplish in the present. Marriage is for life. A healthy marriage is based on love, honesty, respect and the fear of God.

Therefore, it is always better to build your marriage on frankness, truth and trustworthiness. Without a doubt, during the marriage, your spouse will know who you really are. Whenever your spouse discovers your lying game, he or she will have less respect for you. It is going to take you a long time and you will have to take drastic and preventative measures to rebuild that trust.

Marriage is sacred. You will always need God's presence in your marriage. To enjoy fully God's blessing in your marriage, do your best to ensure that the foundation of your marriage is based not on lie and ruse, but on love, honesty, respect and biblical principles.

King Salomon said: "It is better to dwell in the wilderness, than with a contentious and an angry woman" (Proverbs 21: 19). This destructive behavior is wrong for both man and woman. Husband and wife must act respectfully towards each other. Without mutual respect, there will always be fire in their matrimonial life. A few years ago, I was invited to go out with a couple. The husband decided that we go out together in his car; I accepted his proposal. While the husband was driving, we were laughing and making clean jokes. Whenever the husband started to say something, the wife always stopped him by saying: "This is not true. You don't know the story. You are a liar." She put her husband down with a disrespectful tone of voice and took over the story from her husband. At the end, the husband was completely frustrated and embarrassed with the attitude of his wife. He said to his wife:" If you have something to say while I am talking, you must wait until I finish to saying what I am saying instead of stopping me and taking over the conversation".

The conversation suddenly turned into a firestorm of quarrelsome behavior and name-calling. The wife blasted and insulted her husband with all kinds of filthy words and expressions in my presence. I was so shocked to witness that destructive behavior that I didn't say anything for a long period of time. When she came back to her good senses, she apologized to me. But, she didn't apologize to her husband. On the contrary, she blamed her husband for the incident stating that he was responsible for their clash.

Marriage is not a one-way street where one partner is willing to live according to the principles of marriage, and the other one chooses to live without any respect and moral standards. When you buy your favorite car from a car dealer, the seller gives you the car with a manual from the designer of the car. In the manual, you have all the instructions to keep the car in good shape. You know that at a certain moment, you have to perform a complete tune up on the car. Regularly, you should check the basic things in the car, like oil, water and other things. Frequently, you should clean the car inside and out to keep it in good condition.

It is also your responsibility not the designer's to check on a regular basis the tires of your car. If you choose to drive your car without taking care of the basic things in the car, definitely, the car would break down. You will break the car not because it is not a good car, but because of your own negligence. God established the institution of marriage for the delight of the human race. To enjoy healthily the fruition of marriage, both partners must respect the principles of marriage.

Both partners must work together in everything to reach the fulfillment of their marriage healthily. A lot of people are excited about the wedding ceremony. They make all kinds of preparation possible. They are willing to make any sacrifice to make sure that the wedding ceremony is a success at any cost. Marriage is a lifetime sentence. Therefore, use the same determination that you have developed for the success of your wedding ceremony in your matrimonial life for your own happiness. The Christian life is not based on lust, feelings, selfish desires and vicious passions, but on principles.

I knew another couple that was facing many troubles in their marriage. The husband was always on the phone with a female friend. His wife spoke to him many times about it. She told him that she didn't like the direction that he was taking. The husband completely ignored the concern of his wife. That situation created other problems in the family. A few years later, he left his wife to be with his female friend who was in a different state.

When he left his wife, everybody was shocked. But, it was very clear that something like that would have occurred sooner or later. The day that he left the house was not the day that he was separated with his wife. When he decided to develop a deeper emotional bond with his female friend instead of his wife, mentally he was separated from his wife. He was waiting for the appropriate time to physically leave the house. Effectively, he did what he was feeding his mind with.

When you are nourishing something in your mind, it is like a grain that you sow in the ground. If you sow three or four grains of corn on the ground, they will grow. And, they will keep growing until you will be able to reap the fruit of the grains that you have sowed. It is the same thing with your mind. What you sow in your mind will keep growing until you reap its fruit. Your mental attitude is very significant in every single aspect of your life. Your mind-set is very powerful.

Whenever you choose to take a negative direction in your conjugal life to satisfy your selfish desires, you could bring suffering, pain, shame, humiliation, disrespect, sorrow and disappointment not only to your spouse, but also into your own life. Don't deceive yourself by thinking that you can take away the peace of mind of your spouse and live in peace. It doesn't matter if you believe it or not, your actions in your matrimonial life whether secret or not will always follow you. Sooner or later, your secret dishonest adventure in your conjugal life will definitely come to light whether you think about it or not.

Absolutely, there are a lot of things that could produce disastrous consequences in your marriage. Some of them are:

Infidelity

Dishonesty

Immorality

Amorality

Adultery

Disloyalty

Disrespect

Lies

Deceitfulness

Arrogance

Pride

Quarrelsome attitude

Denial

Cheating.

And, you will have to live with their repercussions for the rest of your life. Therefore, take your marriage seriously. For your own welfare and peace of mind, do not destroy your marriage to please your sinful desires, your ex boyfriend / girlfriend or anybody else. For your own happiness, do your best to respect the boundaries in marriage. To avoid the destructive mistakes in marriage mentioned above, you should honestly surrender your life to Jesus Christ; and, you should develop a mental disposition to live morally, honestly to enjoy healthily the rest of your life with your partner.

Chapter 4
Effects Of Infidelity In Marriage

A dishonest, irresponsible and unfaithful man could reason with you and come with all kinds of rational arguments to convince you that morality is a prison.

Martial A. Charles

God created human beings with different kinds of potentialities, faculties and abilities to accomplish marvelous things in life. One of the most powerful gifts that God has bestowed upon the human race is the freedom to choose. With this wonderful gift, we can choose to build different types of bridges in our conjugal life to preserve, protect and secure our marriage. Or, we can choose to build all kinds of walls in our matrimonial life to damage and destroy our marriage. Never forget that each choice in life, whether positive or negative has its outcomes.

To cover up their negative actions and to try to win the sympathy of others, some people call their negative behavior an accident. Others say: "It just happens." In reality, it is not an accident. It doesn't just happen. It is a matter of choice. What I am depicting is not something new. It is a reality of everyday life. Even though we know what is right and what is wrong, whenever we voluntarily choose to please our fleshly desires, we always try to find a way to cover up or to find an excuse for our negative and destructive behavior. This is the tendency of our sinful nature.

Infidelity in marriage is not an accident. It doesn't just happen. It is a choice. Take a few moments to think about it. Those who choose the path of infidelity always start it in secret. They do their best to keep it like that. They don't want their spouse to know about it. They act with their spouse like everything is okay in their relationship. They are willing and always ready to lie and to deny any wrongdoing. They believe that they are very smart by managing to keep their infidelity in secret for a long period of time. However, sooner or later, it will come to light for the whole world to see. There is no doubt it, one day, somehow or somewhere, it will be exposed publicly.

There is an Haitian proverb that states:" The hole of a lie is not too deep." It means, when you lie, one way or another, the truth will surely come out. You cannot hide a lie from everybody forever. Therefore, think and rethink about your own choices in life. In the light of all these transactions to cover up a dishonest behavior, it as clear as day and night that infidelity is not an accident. It is a voluntary and personal choice.

There are different categories of people among those who choose the path of infidelity. Firstly, let 's examine those who grew up in an unstable family. During their childhood, infidelity was the way of life of their parents. It was a part of their environment. Therefore, from their childhood, they were programmed to accept infidelity as a good behavior. If they don't receive any professional help, there is a great possibility that they will start practicing infidelity in their early teen years or in their teenage years. They could become even smarter than their parents in practicing this terrible behavior.

By the way, some of them develop all kinds of strategies to play their own parents in that matter. At home, they behave in a certain way just to convince their parents to believe in them. However, secretly, they have a double life. Before getting married, they already have many years of experience in infidelity. As experts in infidelity, some of them could easily choose to continue to practice infidelity in their matrimonial life. They don't have any problem with cheating on their spouse. It is a part of their specialty. Some of them could use all kinds of arguments to convince their spouse that it is only a simple friendship. This is the reality of those who choose to live in deception.

There are others who grew up in an unstable family where their parents didn't practice infidelity. However, their parents neglected them emotionally, affectionately and tenderly during their infancy. That parental mistake creates a lot of psychological troubles in their lives. There is always a sense of emptiness in their lives. Again, if they don't get any professional help, they will definitely find a way or another to deal with the feeling of emptiness in their own lives.

Unfortunately, one of the harmful ways that most of them choose to fill the emptiness in their lives is illicit sexual exploration. While practicing promiscuity, they feel a sense of relief. Therefore, they use it, and they keep using it as a tool to fix the hole in their lives. They feel very good about it. For them, it is like they find the key of their true identity.

However, this detrimental behavior will never be able to fill the feeling of emptiness in their lives. In reality, they choose the wrong path of life. They are destroying themselves physically, emotionally, mentally, morally, psychologically and spiritually. The worst part of it, when they get married, they bring their hurtful and deceitful habit of infidelity with them.

Secondly, there are some people who grew up in a good

family who choose to live according to the patterns of this world. They choose to reject their moral standards to embrace the sexual revolution of this age. The entertainment industries greatly influence a lot of people all over the world. By watching some programs, you can free of charge and easily learn how to cheat and how to practice infidelity. There are many people around the world who are addicted with these programs. They cannot live without them. They cannot spend a day without watching them. In these programs, they have their own definition of marriage. They promote their own concepts of matrimonial life. They establish their own way of life. They promote and encourage promiscuity and infidelity. Cheating, violence, crime, dishonesty and sexual immorality are elevated to the highest level possible.

Whatever you choose to sow in your mind, you will definitely reap the fruit in the time of harvest. While you are reading this chapter, I would advise you to take some time to think of how you have been influenced by what you are watching, reading and listening to. There are a lot of negative things that you choose to do in your own life because of what you are watching, listening to and reading. How many times do you give up your moral principles to do something that you absolutely know is wrong? How many times do you choose to put aside your core values to adopt the popular inclinations of this world?

There are many people who are promoting the erroneous view that infidelity is the problem of man. It is as though all men are cheaters. It is not true. There are a lot of faithful men all over the world who choose to live honestly and happily with their wives. As some men, there are a lot of women who are also professional cheaters. By the way, some of them are smarter than men in practicing infidelity. By the same token, there are a lot of faithful women on the four corners of the earth who choose to live honestly and happily with their husbands. Infidelity is not the problem of a particular gender.

It is the problem of the entire human race.

Both man and woman have a sinful nature. In our beautiful blue planet, sin does not affect only men. Sin affects both men and women. It is a human tragedy. Both men and women choose to gratify their sinful desires. Both men and women choose to practice infidelity. Let's not try to practice the blame games in that matter. The essential point is that infidelity is a harmful and destructive behavior. It will always bring devastation and painful results. Both husband and wife must do their best to avoid it at any cost if they really want to enjoy their matrimonial life healthily.

Let's take some examples. When you got married, you took a vow to be faithful to your spouse. Suddenly, your ex-boyfriend or girlfriend wants to have an illicit relationship with you. Your boss makes all kinds of advances for you to have a secret and deceitful affair with him or her. When you go out by yourself, you meet a handsome man or a beautiful woman that greatly attracts you; he or she makes himself or herself available to you right away. Your co-worker is pressuring you to have a dishonest affair with him or her. What are your reactions towards those people? Do you keep chatting with them? Do you keep joking with them? Do you keep laughing with them regarding their proposal? Or, do you resolutely reject their immoral proposal? None of those people could make their depraved proposition a reality if you don't choose to accept their shady offer. You have two options. It is whether you accept or reject categorically their decadent proposition.

By the way, those who choose to practice the debauched life with no regard for moral principles are very smart in their dissipated exploration. They systematically observe your reaction, verbal and non-verbal expressions to determine if it is worth it or not to pursue their seduction that will ultimately ruin your matrimonial life and your own life. So, when you say no to infidelity, make sure that you say no firmly to infidelity in all circumstances with a strong will. To protect yourself, and for your own welfare, build a wall in that matter between you and all those who try to seduce you in corrupt relationship. By doing so, you will protect yourself and your entire family from the hefty consequences of infidelity in marriage.

Infidelity in marriage has short-term and long-term consequences. An instant perverted pleasure of infidelity could bring you a lifetime of sorrows, disappointments and catastrophic outcomes. The effects of sexual infidelity are very painful and bring different kinds of destructions. Some of the effects are:

Emotional pain
Psychological troubles
Uncontrolled anger
Humiliation
Depression
Anxiety
Insecurity
Sadness
Stress
Feelings of emptiness
Confusion
Division
Rivalry
Lost of trust
Lost of credibility
Nourishing susceptibility
Hatred
Animosity
Rancor
Reprisal
Detestation
Resentment
Discomfort

Strife
Discord
Annoyance
Outrage
Rage
Grief
Disgrace
Scandal
Panic
Sorrow
Shame
Headache
Trouble
Bitter fruit
Hurting yourself and other people
Destroying your family
Breaking your emotional bond with your spouse
Humiliating your spouse and your children
Destroying your relationship with your spouse
Tarnishing your relationship with your children
Paving the way for your children to follow the same negative
path
Damaging your image
Loss of career
Divorce
Illegitimate birth
Abortion
Unfortunately, sometimes, loss of one's life
Putting the whole family on the line
Risk of contracting STD's
Degradation
Indignation
Agitation
Disorientation
Apprehension

Retaliation
Abomination
Jealousy
Enmity
Fury
Worry
Uncertainty
Unhappiness
Nervousness
Uneasiness
Tenseness
Wretchedness
Disagreement
Embarrassment
Bewilderment
Damaging your relationship with God
Destroying your inner peace
Bringing shame, disrespect and despair in your own life
Self-harm
Self-deception
Self-delusion
Self-destruction.

When we choose to respect the sanctity of marriage, we protect ourselves from the horrible consequences of infidelity. Conversely, when we choose to have lustful relationship, we open the door for calamities to invade our lives. There is no doubt about it; the seeds of sexual infidelity always bring deep emotional scars with unpleasant consequences from generation to generation.

If you are not convinced about the crucial significance of this statement, take some time to read and think deeply about the ongoing dreadful consequences of the sexual infidelity of Abraham and David in the Bible.

The descendants of Abraham are still reaping the seeds of his sexual infidelity. A lot of families all over the world are upside down because of sexual infidelity. We are all sinners. We all make mistakes somehow or somewhere in life. God is love. God is always willing to forgive our sins. When we sincerely repent, we can restore our relationship with God. However, God's forgiveness does not remove the consequences of our sins. Whenever we choose to disobey God's law, we will always pay the consequences.

King David honestly repented for his sexual infidelity. Effectively, God forgave him. But, the consequences of his action were inevitable. Let's take a look at the consequences of David's harmful behavior.

"The sword shall never depart from thy house" (2 Samuel 12: 10).

"I will raise evil out of thy own house" (2 Samuel 12: 11).

"Your sin shall be revealed" (2 Samuel 12: 12).

"The child born unto thee shall die" (2 Samuel 12: 14).

Deliberate disobedience to God's Moral Law and rebellion against God will always produce destruction and calamities with lasting horrible repercussions. On the other hand, loving obedience to God's Law of liberty and a contrite heart will always generate peace, understanding, joy and happiness. There are a lot of negative things that we could avoid in our lives if only we steadfastly determine to make our choices wisely.

Poor judgment and the constant excitement to please self at any cost are the inevitable steps to self-delusion and self-deception. Pride, arrogance, self-importance, self-centeredness, malicious tendencies, disrespect and madness of greatness are the inescapable steps to self-glorification and self-destruction. In contrast, the fear of the Lord, wisdom, sound judgment and Christlike attitude in all circumstances are the key to living in peace with God and your neighbor, and, to protect yourself from the horrendous enduring aftermath of destructive choices in life.

From Genesis to Revelation, the Bible depicts how the Supreme Ruler of the universe has high regard for marriage. There is no doubt about it; marriage is something very special in the eyes of God. It is sacred. If you really want to have a healthy marriage and live happy, you must give the control of your mind, your heart, your will and your thoughts to Jesus Christ. Ellen G. White stated: " Christ presented before His disciples the far-reaching principles of the law of God. He taught His hearers that the law was transgressed by the thoughts before the evil desire was carried out in actual commission. We are under obligation to control our thoughts, and to bring them into subjection to the law of God. The noble powers of the mind have been given to us by the Lord, that we may employ them in contemplating heavenly things. God has made abundant provision that the soul may make continual progression in the divine life…. We give our time and thought to the trivial and commonplace things of the world, and neglect the great interests that pertain to eternal life." –The SDA Bible Commentary, Vol. 3, p. 1145.

Self-examination Questionnaire For Personal Inventory In Your Matrimonial Life

Please, take your time to examine your own life, and write down your own resolution. Do not think about other people. Honestly and healthily, scrutinize yourself.

Have I founded my marriage on honesty or on lies?

My resolution:

Have I been playing games with my spouse from the beginning of our relationship?

My resolution:

Have I purposely lie about my past relationships just to get married?
My resolution:

Have I purposely presented myself as an angel just to get married?
My resolution:

Have I kept secretly my relationship with my ex-boyfriend/
girlfriend?
My resolution:

Have I been dishonest with my spouse?
My resolution:

Have I purposely deceived my spouse from time to time?
My resolution:

Have I been acting faithfully in everything with my spouse?
My resolution:
Have I been lying to my spouse?
My resolution:

Am I very comfortable deceiving my spouse?
My resolution:

Have I being respectful to my spouse?
My resolution:

Have I been disrespectful to my spouse?
My resolution:

Have I been treating my spouse with respect and dignity?
My resolution:

Have I been treating my spouse as a second -class citizen?

My resolution:

Have I been treating my ex-boyfriend/girlfriend with more respect than my spouse?

My resolution:

Have I been giving priority to my so-called friendship with my ex-boyfriend/girlfriend than my relationship with my spouse?

My resolution:

Have I been very disrespectful to my spouse just to keep my so-called friendship with my boyfriend/girlfriend?

My resolution:

Have I spent more time, talking, chatting, flirting, and networking with my ex-boyfriend/girlfriend and so- called social network friends than with my spouse?

My resolution:

Have I respected my marriage boundaries and my commitment to my spouse?

My resolution:

Have I introduced my ex-boyfriend/girlfriend to my spouse as a simple friend or a brother in the church?

My resolution:

Have I reacted disrespectfully with my spouse when he or she knows about my relationship with my ex-boyfriend/girlfriend?

My resolution:

Did I sincerely apologize to my spouse?

My resolution:

Or, did I try to play games as usual by acting like it was nothing more than a simple friendship?

My resolution:

Have I been lying to my spouse about my job just to spend more time secretly with my ex-boyfriend/girlfriend?

My resolution:

Am I very reluctant to give my job phone number to my spouse while I have already given it, including my job address, to my ex-boyfriend/girlfriend?

My resolution:

What is my intention in lying to my spouse about my job phone number?

My resolution:

What is my main goal in lying to my spouse and giving my job phone number, address and e-mail to my ex-boyfriend/girlfriend?

My resolution:

Am I taking my marriage seriously?

My resolution:

Am I taking my relationship with my spouse seriously?

My resolution:

Why have I chosen to live in ruse and lies?

My resolution:

Am I really happy by living a double life?

My resolution:

For how long will my spouse tolerate me?
My resolution:

Am I being honest to myself?
My resolution:

Am I helping my marriage?
My resolution:

Or, am I destroying my own marriage?
My resolution:

Am I living selfishly, dishonestly and destructively?
My resolution:

Will my marriage survive?
My resolution:

Are there consequences for my misleading behavior?
My resolution:

Why am I doing whatever I want in my marriage?
My resolution:

Why am I ignoring my spouse's concerns in our marriage?
My resolution:

Why have I decided to do whatever and to go wherever I want without consulting my spouse?
My resolution:

Why am I not listening to my spouse?
My resolution:

Why have I decided to satisfy my own feelings regardless of my spouse's displeasure?
My resolution:

Why have I decided to make my decision without first talking to my spouse?
My resolution:

Why did I choose not to submit to my husband loving leadership as stated in the Bible?
My resolution:

Why did I choose not to collaborate with my spouse?
My resolution:

Why did I choose to be unfaithful and disrespectful to my spouse?
My resolution:

Why did I choose to cultivate resentment against my spouse?
My resolution:

Could my cunning actions and reactions in my marriage reach a point of no return?
My resolution:

What about my relationship with God, my well-being and my eternal life?
My resolution:
My commitment to be a faithful and responsible spouse:
My prayer to God:

Chapter 5
Steps To A Healthy Marriage

An honest, respectful, responsible Christian woman is priceless. She reflects God's character in her conjugal life by the power of the Holy Spirit. She is sweeter than honey and sugar. She is more delicious than all the delicious fruits on planet earth. She submits herself and cooperates healthily, lovingly, obediently, voluntarily and respectfully with her husband for the happiness of their marriage and their own well-being in this world and the world to come.

Martial A. Charles

There are many people all over the world who have never seen an oven. They have no clue about it. Some of you may say: how and where do they cook their food? Well, they have a way to cook their food. It is a pleasure to sit down at a table to eat food. However, we should also remember that there are steps to follow to get the food on the table. In some places in the world, they use three average stones to cook their food instead of an oven. These three stones play a fundamental role. While preparing the food, if you move one stone, there will be chaos and disaster.

The pan cannot and would not stand on two stones. As soon as you move a stone, the pan would fall. In these places, if you want to sit down at a table to eat your food joyfully, you must prepare it on three stones. It is the same thing for marriage. A healthy marriage stands and depends on three persons. The first Person is the Supreme Moral Being of the Cosmos who is the Founder and the Sustainer of marriage. The other two persons are the husband and his wife. The husband should have a deep relationship with God and his wife. The wife should also have a deep relationship with God and her husband.

Based on the above example, we can firmly declare that marriage constitutes a divine- human triangle. God, the husband, and the wife form a loving triangle. Marriage is sacred. Even those who claim that they don't believe in God, when they make up their mind to have a healthy marriage, the Holy Spirit guides them in the right direction. We are born in sin. We are all in need of God's help in our marriage.

Therefore, all human beings have a sinful nature. And also, we are all created in God's image. Even if we have a sinful nature, God created us with a level of morality and the ability to choose what direction we want to take with our lives. He or she who earnestly wants to have a healthy marriage has at his or her disposal all the tools to make it a reality. There are different types of steps to having a healthy marriage. Let's analyze some of them.

Step 1: You must make the choice to give the control of your mind, your will and your heart to Jesus Christ.

When you make that decision, you say to yourself, to God and to the world that you choose to live morally, honestly and obediently to God's ordinances with the help and the guidance of the Holy Spirit. So, it is your responsibility to close the gates, the doors and the windows of your mind from the desires of your sinful nature that are contrary to the will of

God. You may ask yourself the question: what is this preacher talking about? I am going to clarify it for you.

Let me take a simple example. You are living in a beautiful house. The house is well protected. You place the most sophisticated cameras all over the house. You install the best alarm system in the house. You place a big gate in front of the house. You know that there are robbers, criminal, crazy people and wild animals in this world. So, you do all these things to protect yourself. At night, you check all the doors of the house to make sure that they are closed.

No one can get inside your house without your permission. When you invite someone into your house, you open the gate to let the person in. You open the door and you receive the person into your living room. When the visit is over, you reopen the gate for the visitor to get out. As soon as your guest goes through the gate, you close it. Therefore, there is no way for an outsider to get inside your house without your invitation.

There are different places in your house. You receive your friends and visitors in your living room. When you invite them to eat with you in your house, you invite them to eat in your dining room. If you invite them to sleep in your house, you put them in your guest rooms. There are many other rooms in the house. Each room in the house is used for something specific. There are limits for each room. Anybody cannot go anywhere in your house as he or she wishes without your approval.

Finally, you have your bedroom. Your bedroom is a restricted place in your house that is reserved for you and your spouse to sleep and to act as husband and wife. Your bedroom is the special place in your house where you have your intimate clothes and you know very well the rest. So, it is completely impossible for an outsider to go to your bedroom that you know belongs only to you and your partner without your full consent. Unfortunately, many people are doing just that every single day. I am using this illustration to help you understand how your mind functions including the effects of your choices in your own life.

When you get married, you know for sure that you have to be faithful and honest in everything with your spouse. You know that your spouse must be your best friend, your partner and your lover. You know that you must respect the restricted areas in your marriage. You are fully aware that you must respect the boundaries in marriage. You know that you must develop your deepest emotional bond only for your spouse after Jesus Christ. You know for sure that these things and many more belong only to your partner, not your ex-boyfriend/girlfriend or anybody else.

However, if you choose to live in pleasing the desires of your sinful nature that are in rebellion against the moral principles, you will definitely reap the fruit of your own choices. Whether you choose to live under the influence of the Holy Spirit or not, everything starts in your mind. When you get married, you don't just get up in the morning and start flirting and having secret relationship with your ex or somebody else.

You act according to your state of mind. You first conceive it in your mind. You then convince yourself that it is okay. You make your own choice to put on pause your own morality to do something that you absolutely know is not the right thing to do. Even if you know internally that you are heading in a destructive way, you choose to go for it. You plan your dishonest adventure in secrecy.

The reason why you do it secretly is because you know in your inner soul, that what you choose to do is completely wrong. But to satisfy your selfish and sinful passions, you do it anyway. Satan deceived Eve in the Garden of Eden not because she didn't know that what she was doing was wrong, but because of her own mindset. She knew very well that she should be always connected with her husband physically, mentally and emotionally. She knew very well that she should always be connected with God mentally and spiritually. It was her choice to disconnect herself mentally from God and emotionally from her husband.

As soon as she created that empty space in her mind, Satan took full advantage of her own choice right away. And, you know the destructive consequences of her secret deceitful exploration. When you get married, you should always control the gates, the doors and the windows of your mind. The gates, the doors and the windows symbolize the different ways that you allow certain things to reach your mind. When they reach your mind, you choose where you want to place them.

For example, your ex boyfriend/girlfriend and some of your opposite sex friends, could be very curious and fascinated to ask you questions about your sexual life with your spouse. In the next move, they could also try to convince you to have illicit and secret relationship with them.

It is your responsibility to choose if you want to place them where they belong, or if you want to open the doors of your mind and discuss with them things that you absolutely know that you should only discuss with your partner. If you choose to place them in their own territory, you close the gates of your mind to never come back to that subject with them. And, you must make up your mind to keep them away from you in that matter.

Absolutely, you do the right thing to protect your relationship with God, your own well-being, your respect, your relationship with your partner and the boundaries in your marriage. However, if you choose to accept their dishonest adventure, you open the doors of your mind for them to cultivate their destructive seed. You make your own choice to open the doors of your mind to let them in. Never forget that your deceitful choices will always bring their disastrous consequences. They walk together. You won't see the consequences right away, but they will surely come at the appropriate time.

Dishonest choices in marriage will greatly affect your communion with God. They will break your moral principles. They will tarnish your relationship and your image with your spouse. They could lead you to cross the limits of your marriage. Definitely, they will create different types of troubles in your own life. So, do not choose to put yourself in dangerous territory.

Be strong in your decision to keep away your ex boyfriend/ girlfriend, co-worker and friend who are trying to have dishonest relationship with you. If you open the doors of your mind to let them in, they are not going to stay in the living room of your mind inactively. In their mind, they already know exactly where they want to be. While they are in the living room of your mind, they will do whatever they can to convince you to allow them to spend a few minutes in the bedroom of your mind.

Once they reach that point, they have accomplished their illicit mission. And, you are the loser. Above all, you will have to live with the scars of your deceiving exploration for the rest of your life. I have seen a lot of examples.

Many years ago, I was watching a TV program in which there were several women who were talking about their first love. The talk show host asked one of the women: "How did you meet your first love?" She was laughing, and she said: "Well, it was an accident. It just happened. We were friends. We used to talk about everything on the phone. One day, he came over to my house. I was alone, it just happened."

Is it really true that it was an accident? Let us briefly analyze her argument. According to her own affirmation, the guy was her friend. They never officially changed their friendship to the level of even boyfriend and girlfriend.

However, in their conversation, they already acted

as husband and wife. There were no boundaries in their conversation. There are things that you could discuss with your friends. There are things to discuss with your boyfriend and girlfriend. And, there are things that you should only discuss with your spouse. There are things that you could do with your friend. There are things that you could do with your boyfriend and girlfriend, not your friend. And, there are things that you should do only with your spouse, not your friend or boyfriend/girlfriend.

So, the action that she committed with her friend instead of her husband started a long time ago in her mind. Therefore, it was not an accident. It was the direct result of her choice to live with no boundaries with her friend. When she opened the gates, the doors and the windows of her mind to her friend, she should clearly establish the limits for her friend. She didn't give him any restriction.

She gave him the permission to live in the guest room of her mind. While he was in the guest room, he diligently made his way to be with her in the bedroom of her mind. She voluntarily accepted the offer in her mind. So, at the right time, she ate physically the fruit of what she cultivated in her mind. When you get married, if you choose to put yourself in the same position, there is no doubt about it; you could get the same result. Therefore, it is your responsibility to be vigilant to protect the different avenues of your mind. Whatever you choose to cultivate in your mind would bring its fruit sooner or later in your life. If you cultivate something positive in your mind, it will bring positive fruit. If you cultivate something negative in your mind, it will certainly bring negative fruit in your life.

There is a big difference between those who choose to live as they want and those who choose to live according to the word of God. The apostle Paul affirmed: "For those who live according to the flesh set their minds on the things of the flesh, but those who live according to the Spirit, the things of the

Spirit. For to be carnally minded is death; but to be spiritually minded is life and peace. Because the carnal mind is enmity against God; for it is not subject to the law of God, nor indeed can be. So then, those who are in the flesh cannot please God. But you are not in the flesh but in the Spirit, if indeed the spirit of God dwells in you. Now if anyone does not have the Spirit of Christ, he is not His. And if Christ is in you, the body is dead because of sin, but the Spirit is life because of righteousness. But if the Spirit of Him who raised Jesus from the dead dwells in you, He who raised Christ from the dead will also give life to your mortal bodies through His Spirit who dwells in you" (Romans 8: 5-11).

To enjoy healthily your Christian life and your marriage, you should conquer your sinful desires. The only key to triumph over your sinful desires is to make the choice to live by the power of the Holy Spirit. The apostle Paul knew and experienced very well this vital principal. He declared: "So, I say, let the Holy Spirit guide your life. Then you won't be doing what your sinful nature craves. The sinful nature wants to do evil, which is just the opposite of what the Spirit wants. And the Spirit give us desires that are the opposite of what the sinful nature desires" (Galatians 5: 16-17).

Step 2: You must be willing to develop a healthy relationship with your spouse.

Again, to make this principle a reality in your life, your mental attitude is a must to realize it. You have to make up your mind that you want to live healthily with your partner in every single aspect of your life. Before going further, let me tell you that marriage is the beginning of a lifetime journey.

A lot of people consider marriage as the pinnacle of their life journey. This concept would lead to negligence, carelessness, lack of focus and many other things. Marriage is not the same thing as your graduation at University. On the contrary, marriage is like when you start going to school. It is a long way from kindergarten to University.

However, marriage is completely longer than the period from kindergarten to University. Your marriage graduation has no time limit. Marriage is the beginning of a new life. Marriage is a life sentence. Therefore, you should not take God's blessing, your partner and your marriage for granted. You know the difference between right and wrong. Absolutely, you know the big difference between good and evil.

Internally, you know what is right and you know what is wrong. Stop pleasing your natural tendencies to play games. Instead of playing games with your own life, I advise you to discipline your mind. Be honest with God, yourself, your partner and in everything you do in life. Always communicate and discuss everything together with your spouse. Seek together God's presence and blessing in your marriage. After Jesus Christ, be deeply connected emotionally only with your partner.

Step 3: You must make up your mind to eat apple until death only from your delicious apple tree.

"Drink water from your own cistern, and running water from your own well. Should your fountains be dispersed abroad, streams of water in the street? Let them be only your own, and not for strangers with you. Let your fountain be blessed and rejoice with the wife of your youth" (Proverbs 5:15-18).

When you get married, God gives you a well for life. Whenever you are thirsty, drink from your well. There is always water in the well. So, focus your mind on your own well. Drink and keep drinking from your well. When you get married, you receive a life sentence to enjoy yourself sexually only with your spouse.

King Solomon said: "Enjoy life with the wife whom you love, all the days of your vain life that he has given you under the sun, because that is your portion in life and in your toil at which you toil under the sun" (Ecclesiastes 9: 9).

The husband must fulfill his sexual desires only with his wife. The wife must fulfill her sexual desires only with her husband. It is a sacred duty. It is a must. It is a divine mandate. Excuses and pretext are not a justification for breaking it. It is always a personal choice. Therefore, I encourage you to make the right choice for your own well-being to enjoy yourself sexually only with your spouse for the rest of your life.

Step 4: You must treat your spouse with love, respect, dignity and affection.

"Wives, submit yourselves unto your own husbands, as unto the Lord; for the husband is the head of the wife, even as Christ is the head of the church, and He is the savior of the body. Therefore as the church is subject unto Christ, so let the wives be to their own husbands in every thing. Husbands, love your wives even as Christ also loved the church and gave Himself for it" (Ephesians 5:22-25). Unfortunately, there are a lot of men all over the world who have used and are using this passage to treat their wives as they wish.

According to the Bible, man and woman are created in the image of God. They are created equal. God performed a surgery in Adam's body. He took one of Adam's ribs and made Eve (Genesis 2: 21-22). Eve was a part of Adam. The difference is that men and women do not have the same role and function. The husband is the priest of the family. He is the leader of the family. The husband should always protect his wife and treat her in a special way.

Effectively, she is very special. She is the most beautiful creature on planet earth. You should be excited to have your wife at your side. God places her beside you as your helper until you die. Your wife is your companion for life. It is with your wife that you can enjoy lovingly, fully, morally and legally the gift of procreation.

The wife must lovingly and voluntarily submit herself to her husband. She must collaborate with him in order that they can establish an atmosphere of love, peace, joy and mutual respect for the happiness of the whole family.

In God's plan for husband and wife, there is no room for commanding your wife as a tyrant to obey your order. This philosophy has nothing to do with the word of God. In some places in the world, the husband considers and treats his wife as a maid. This concept comes from the human wisdom. It does not come from God's ordinances regarding marriage.

Instead of always giving orders to your wife, do your best to use your leadership skills properly not to hurt your wife, but to treat her with love. There are a lot of basic things that are very significant. For example, instead of saying: I want you to do this or that, it would be nicer to say: please, can you do this or that for me? And, always say thank you. Show your affection and your appreciation to your wife by your words and your actions.

On the other hand, there are a lot of women who do not want to hear about God's command to submit themselves to their husbands. They have no respect for their husbands. They choose to follow their selfish desires and the patterns of this world that are in complete contradiction with the word of God. Some of them act like they are in a competition for revenge, power, dominion, superiority and greatness. Others choose to satisfy their desires and feelings by any means without any regard for moral principles and marriage boundaries.

God didn't establish the marriage institution for competition, dissension, self-glorification, self-exaltation and self- gratification. The Maker of heaven and earth created the institution of marriage for completion, collaboration, cooperation, union, communion, affection and sanctification between husband and wife. Therefore, the wife must always do her best to treat her husband with respect and dignity. She should lovingly submit herself to her husband.

Ellen G. White declared: "We must have the Spirit of God, or we can never have harmony in the home. The wife, if she has the spirit of Christ, will be careful of her words; she will control her spirit, she will be submissive, and yet will not feel that she is a bondslave, but a companion to her husband. If the husband is a servant of God, he will not lord it over his wife; he will not be arbitrary and exacting. We cannot cherish home affection with too much care; for the home, if the Spirit of the Lord dwells there, is a type of heaven. . . . If one errs, the other will exercise Christlike forbearance and not draw coldly away.

Neither the husband nor the wife should attempt to exercise over the other an arbitrary control. Do not try to compel each other to yield to your wishes. You cannot do this and retain each other's love. Be kind, patient, and forbearing, considerate, and courteous. By the grace of God you can succeed in making each other happy, as in your marriage vow you promised to do."

Step 5: Do not cultivate bitterness against your partner.

"In your anger do not sin. Do not let the sun go down while you are still angry" (Ephesians 4: 26). To enjoy healthily your marriage and your Christian life in general, you should be able to control your emotions. If you let your emotions control you, you put yourself on the wrong path. How is your relationship with your partner? Are you in control of your anger while you are living with your spouse? It is very important to analyze and think about these questions. Uncontrolled anger could create a lot of troubles in your own life and in your marriage.

If your partner does something wrong, it is always better to discuss the matter with your spouse in a peaceful way instead of nourishing anger and bitterness in your mind. You are hurting yourself. Internally, you are not at peace. Sometimes, you will act in a negative way towards your partner for no reason. It is the consequence of your own state of mind. From time to time, you will behave in a strange way. Internally, you might consider your strange behavior as a way that you are punishing your partner.

On the contrary, you are punishing yourself. Your spouse cannot read your mind. He or she doesn't know what's going on in your mind. Internally, if there is something that is bothering you, it would be totally wiser to discuss it with your spouse in a peaceful way. By cultivating resentment against your spouse for something wrong he or she has done in the past that you didn't like, you are destroying your own life. I would encourage you to discuss the matter respectfully with your partner, and, move forward healthily with your life.

Therefore, the best thing to do is to discuss what is troubling you with your partner in a peaceful way. The sooner you choose to discuss it respectfully with your partner, the better for your own well-being, your relationship with God and your relationship with your spouse. So, calm down. Take a deep breath. Take a walk in the yard or in the neighborhood. When you let your anger control you, you could disconnect yourself to God easily. Whenever you disconnect yourself with God, you open the door for Satan to use your disconnection from God to bring division and other troubles in your own life and your marriage.

According to Ellen G. White: "If the will of God is fulfilled, the husband and wife will respect each other and cultivate love and confidence. Anything that would mar the peace and unity of the family should be firmly repressed, and kindness and love should be cherished. He who manifests the spirit of tenderness, forbearance, and love will find that the same spirit will be reflected upon him. Where the Spirit of God reigns, there will be no talk of unsuitability in the marriage relation. If Christ indeed is formed within, the hope of glory, there will be union and love in the home. Christ abiding in the heart of the wife will be at agreement with Christ abiding in the heart of the husband. They will be striving together for the mansions Christ has gone to prepare for those who love Him." So, pray and ask God to help you to control your anger and your sinful desires through the power of the Holy Spirit in order that you can enjoy healthily your marriage and your Christian life joyously.

Step 6: You should prove that you love your spouse through your deeds and your words.

"In the same way, you husbands must give honor to your wives. Treat your wives with understanding as you live together. She may be weaker than you are, but she is your equal partner in God's gift of new life. Treat her as you should so your prayers will not be hindered" (1 Peter 3: 7).

As the spiritual leader of the family, the husband must reflect God's image in the way that he treats his wife. If you don't want to jeopardize your relationship with God, treat your wife affectionately and lovingly. Marriage is not a game. Marriage is not something to take lightly. Both the husband and his wife should take seriously their marriage and do their best to create an atmosphere of love, honesty, respect and affection.

Both the husband and his wife are accountable to God for the way that they choose to treat each other. "Wives, in the same way be submissive to your husbands so that if any of them do not believe the word, they may be won over without words by the behavior of their wives" (1 Peter 3: 1). This is not a matter of superiority and inferiority; on the contrary, this requirement is for the happiness and the methodical development of the family.

Step 7: You must spend significant time with your spouse.

Marriage is a lifetime commitment. You are responsible for making plans to spend considerable time with your partner. Negligence in that matter can be disastrous. It doesn't matter how demanding your profession is; you should spend time with your partner.

Whenever you choose to neglect your spouse, you create an empty space in your matrimonial life. This empty space could be filled at any time in various unfortunate forms. It is always better to apply the prevention principles in your conjugal life.

Spending time with your partner will greatly contribute to the maturity of your relationship with your spouse. There are some religious people who think that it a sign of spirituality to neglect their wives. They believe that they are so spiritual they don't have time for romance. They don't spend time with their wives. They don't take them out. They don't bring any creativity into their marriage. Romantically and intimately, they neglect their wives. This concept has nothing to do with spirituality.

On the contrary, the husband has a divine mandate to take care of his wife physically, spiritually, emotionally, intimately, romantically and sexually. When you neglect your wife on these levels, you bring sorrow, suffering, frustration, anxiety, anger, hostility, stress, worry, sadness and despair in her life. Even if she doesn't say anything, she is suffering internally. Maybe, you don't know that a woman who is suffering internally romantically could explode at any moment. There are many ways that she could be exploded. Her explosion could bring devastating consequences. A simple look in her face will tell you that she is not happy at all. So, take care of your wife on all the levels mentioned above.

You should create an environment to make her happy. This is your responsibility to make her happy. God created her to be happy. Therefore, she deserves to be happy. Do your job, and accomplish your marital mission faithfully and efficiently. I assure you that your marriage will be stronger than ever. The face of your wife will change completely. By doing so, you will bring love, joy, peace, happiness and satisfaction into the life of your wife. And, your matrimonial life will be exciting, fun, joyous and mature.

Step 8: Be willing to always forgive each other.

"Be kind and compassionate to one another, forgiving each other, just as in Christ God forgave you" (Ephesians 4:32). Contrary to the world concept of marriage, a forgiving attitude would save a marriage and avoid long term suffering for the children and the parents. Sometimes, your teeth hurt your tongue. However, they continue to live in the same place without any problem. A forgiving attitude is medicine for your own health. Keep practicing it in your matrimonial life for the positive development of your marriage.

So, for your own happiness, I advise you to put aside your negative anger against your spouse and apply forgiveness, kindness and tenderness towards each other.

For your own inner serenity, forgive your spouse.

For your own inner serenity, forgive yourself.

For your own inner serenity, eliminate your hatred against your spouse.

For your own inner serenity, throw away your animosity against your spouse.

For your own inner serenity, give up your rancor against your spouse.

For your own inner serenity, reject your grudges against your spouse.

For your own inner serenity, expel your loathing against your spouse.

For your own inner serenity, dismiss your bitterness against your spouse.

For your own inner serenity, discharge your acrimony against your spouse.

For your own inner serenity, eject your hostility against your spouse.

For your own inner serenity, subtract your revenge against your spouse.

For your own inner serenity, take off your reprisal against your spouse.

For your own inner serenity, demolish your moroseness against your spouse.

For your own inner serenity, carry away your resentment against your spouse.

For your own inner serenity, wipe out your detestation against your spouse.

For your own inner serenity, exterminate your rivalry against your spouse.

For your own inner serenity, stamp out your antipathy against your spouse.

For your own inner serenity, bring to an end your wrath against your spouse.

For your own inner serenity, divert yourself of dislike against your spouse.

For your own inner serenity, do away with grouchiness against your spouse.

For your own inner serenity, obliterate your abhorrence against your spouse.

For your own inner serenity, annihilate your sullenness against your spouse.

For your own inner serenity, remove your antagonism against your spouse.

For your own inner serenity, make peace with God and your spouse.

There is no way to find absolute inner serenity in this world with its various scientific, philosophical and metaphysical concepts. True inner serenity is beyond the human realm. Only the redemptive work of Jesus Christ brings total well-being and true inner serenity. Inner rest of spirit is found only in fellowship with the Creator of the cosmos. True inner serenity is a gift from God. We cannot and will never find it anywhere else.

You must forgive the unforgivable to enjoy your peace of mind.

"It is harder to make amends with an offended friend than to capture a fortified city. Arguments separate friends like a gate locked with iron bars" (Proverbs 18: 19).

You must forgive the unforgivable to have a healthy relationship with God.

"But when you are praying, first forgive anyone you are holding a grudge against, so that your Father in heaven will forgive your sins, too" (Mark 11: 25).

You must forgive the unforgivable to repeat the Lord's Prayer.

"And forgive us our sins, just as we have forgiven those who have sinned against us" (Matthew 6: 12a).

You must forgive the unforgivable to receive God's forgiveness.

"If you forgive those who sin against you, your heavenly Father will forgive you. But if you refuse to forgive others, your Father will not forgive your sins" (Matthew 6: 12-15).

You must forgive the unforgivable before bringing your offerings to the altar.

"If you know that someone has something against you, you must reconcile with him or her before offering your sacrifice to God" (Matthew 5: 23-25).

You must continuously forgive the unforgivable.

There is no limit of your forgiveness to those who hurt you (Matthew 18: 21-22).

Therefore, forgive those who wrong you and forgive yourself to be healed from all your emotional scars.

"A cheerful heart is good medicine, but a crushed spirit dries up the bones" (Proverbs 17: 22).

You must follow the example of Jesus on the cross.

While Jesus was in agony, He forgave His enemies (Luke 23: 34).

Step 9: Participate in the household activities.

According to some cultural concepts, the household activities belong to women. When I was in Boston, I used to preach on several religious radio programs. Therefore, many people in that community know me. During a beautiful summer, while my wife was at work, I took all the dirty clothes in the house to a public laundry to wash them. A few minute later, a lady came in to wash her clothes.

When she saw me, she asked: "What are you doing here?" I replied, I am washing my clothes. She exclaimed: "You are a Pastor and you bring your clothes and the clothes of your wife to wash. I can't believe it. I am going to call my husband to see this. My husband never participates in any household activities. He told me that these things belong only to women. Definitely, I am going home to ask my husband to come here to see you."

Effectively, she went home and came back with her husband. It is nice for the husband to participate in the household activities. Your wife will greatly appreciate your participation in the household activities in a degree that you don't even think about. Do not give to your wife the impression that she is your maid. She is not. You should create an environment where she can enjoy what she is doing and be assured that you are with her as your partner in everything.

Step 10: Lovingly, kindly and respectfully, help each other.

Unfortunately, there are some couples that use the intellectual weakness of their partner to humiliate them. Congratulations and excellent job to those who motivate and help their spouse to fill the gap of their intellectual weakness.

Instead of using your partner's inability to put him or her down, you should help him or her to develop his or her potential to accomplish great things in life. If you have a higher education than your spouse, it would be completely better to help him or her to reach a certain level instead of humiliating him or her.

There was a couple that was in that situation. The wife had graduated from college. The husband didn't have a High School Diploma. Joyously, she accepted to marry him. A few years later, she started to put her husband down in front of her friends. She didn't encourage him to go to school. She chose to minimize him. That negative action created other problems in their conjugal life. They didn't seek any professional help. The situation worsened; unfortunately, they are no more together. Husband and wife should help each other in everything for their own happiness.

Step 11: Positively, support and encourage each other.

Some people believe that they should support their spouse only when they are accomplishing something great. No, you should support your partner in small and great things. There are many ways that you could support each other. Your presence is very important. A word of encouragement will be appreciated.

Whatever role you can play, go for it. Your support to your partner is more important than the support of all other persons. Your loving support to your partner has a lasting impact in his or her life. Show your partner that you are connected with him or her by your actions. Husband and wife should take joy in each other's achievements.

Step 12: Keep dating your partner and make of your matrimonial life an exciting journey.

The wedding ceremony is not the completion of your dating skills. If you consider it like that, you will miss the essence of courtship. On the contrary, when you get married, you should keep developing more skills than ever before to continuously date your spouse. It is a lifetime journey. Keep yourself busy with your partner. Continually dating your spouse is one of the best ways to enjoy life with your partner.

Conjugal life is wonderful. It is your responsibility to invent all kinds of ways to keep drinking the pure nectar of your matrimonial juice until you die. Use your imagination and creativity to make your matrimonial life a lifetime journey of love, kindness, fun, admiration and appreciation.

Step 13: Accept and respect the roles and differences of each other.

When you take the nuptial vow with your sweetheart, you become husband and wife. Even if you are husband and wife, you still have different personality and temperament. All the other differences between man and woman remain the same. Physically and biologically, man is different from woman. And also, husband and wife come from different backgrounds, childhood experiences, family environments and life experiences.

Therefore, acceptance and respect of the roles and

differences of each other constitute a fundamental step for the harmonious development of your conjugal life. If you follow carefully this step, it will help you to avoid a lot of headaches, calamities, foolishness and disrespectful behavior in your marriage.

Step 14: Develop a mental attitude to always solve your conflicts healthily.

A healthy marriage doesn't mean a marriage that has no conflict at all. Conversely, a healthy marriage is a marriage where both husband and wife cultivate a mental attitude to always solve their conflict healthily. By solving your conflict in a healthy way, your marriage will become much stronger. Here are some guidelines:

Your spouse is your first neighbor.

Think first before saying anything.

Think first before reacting.

Respect your spouse even in your anger.

Because you are angry, that doesn't give you a license to disrespect your spouse.

Because you are angry, that doesn't give you a permit for any negative words to come out of your mouth against your spouse.

Discipline yourself to manifest respect, understanding and sound judgment.

Be mentally fit.

Be emotionally fit.

Be psychologically fit.

Be spiritually fit.

Be lovingly fit.

Keep your calm.

Inspire confidence instead of being out of control.

Be a good model instead of an adversary.

Be a peacemaker instead of a troublemaker.

Be honest instead of living in denial and ruse.

Be nice instead of being rude.

Be kind instead of being disrespectful.

Be gentle instead of being boorish.

Be tender instead of being discourteous.

Be temperate instead of being impolite.

Be polite instead of being ill-mannered.

Be mindful of the feelings and needs of your spouse.

Be well-mannered with your spouse.

Be always respectful to your spouse.

Avoid addressing filthy and cheeky responses to your spouse.

Always honor your matrimonial commitment even if you are angry.

Identify the problem.

Deal with the problem instead of acting disrespectfully toward your spouse.

Be aware of your non-verbal actions and reactions.

Listen to each other.

Communicate properly, respectfully and lovingly.

Solve your conflict healthily.

Come up with a healthy solution.

Step 15: Surrender totally your mind, your will and your heart to Jesus Christ.

Daily devotion, Bible study, Christ-centered meditation, spiritual, mental cleansing based on biblical principles, and the conviction to live happily, honestly, respectfully, faithfully and morally are the foundation to enjoying healthily your marriage.

For your happiness and your entire family, reject the double life philosophy.

For your happiness and your entire family, renounce secret relationships.

For your own happiness and your entire family, give up to your lustful passions.

For your own happiness and your entire family, let go of self-centeredness.

For your own happiness and your entire family, release yourself from cheating.

For your own happiness and your entire family, loose yourself from flirting adventure.

For your own happiness and your entire family, unleash yourself from trick.

For your own happiness and your entire family, free yourself from ruse.

For your own happiness and your entire family, unshackle yourself from deceitful intents.

For your own happiness and your entire family, liberate yourself from lies.

For your own happiness and your entire family, discharge yourself from dishonesty.

For your own happiness and your entire family, unchain yourself from infidelity.

For your own happiness and your entire family, preserve yourself from immorality.

For your own happiness and your entire family, relinquish promiscuity.

For your own happiness and your entire family, dump irresponsibility.

For your own happiness and your entire family, expel carelessness.

For your own happiness and your entire family, dismiss impoliteness.

For your own happiness and your entire family, get rid of boorishness.

For your own happiness and your entire family, throw away rudeness.

For your own happiness and your entire family, embrace kindness.

For your own happiness and your entire family, protect the windows of your mind.

For your own happiness and your entire family, develop a godly character.

For your own happiness and your entire family, cultivate a healthy attitude.

For your own happiness and your entire family, solve your conflicts healthily.

For your own happiness and your entire family, be always respectful.

For your own happiness and your entire family, collaborate with your partner.

For your own happiness and your entire family, cherish your spouse.

For your own happiness and your entire family, be truthful and honest.

For your own happiness and your entire family, discipline your tongue.

For your own happiness and your entire family, speak with courtesy and respect.

For your own happiness and your entire family, demolish the walls in your marriage.

For your own happiness and your entire family, halt treating your spouse as an adversary.

For your own happiness and your entire family, team up with your partner.

For your own happiness and your entire family, cooperate with each other.

For your own happiness and your entire family, compliment each other.

For your own happiness and your entire family, work together with your partner.

For your own happiness and your entire family, honor your commitment to your spouse.

For your own happiness and your entire family, keep reiterating your love for your partner.

For your own happiness and your entire family, keep building bridges in your marriage.

For your own happiness and your entire family, make of Jesus the center of your life.

For your own happiness and your entire family, make of Jesus the Cornerstone of your marriage.

Step 16: Tear down the walls in your marriage.

There are many ways to build walls in your marriage. Those walls can turn your matrimonial life upside down mentally, emotionally, psychologically, spiritually and physically. How many walls do you build in your marriage? Do you build them to show your partner how great you are? Do you build them just to satisfy your deceitful intents? Or, do you build them by ignorance?

Unfortunately, there are a lot of couples on the four corners of the earth that choose to build walls in their marriage by pride, self-gratification and ignorance. Are you willing to demolish the walls that you put up in your marriage? Allow me to tell you that the motivation, the effort, the energy, the enthusiasm, the determination and the wisdom to pull down the walls that you choose to put up in your marriage are priceless.

However, your refusal to destroy the walls that you choose to put up in your own marriage will always come with a heavy price with lasting and dreadful consequences. Take a simple look in our sinful world; you will clearly see the reality in a daily manner. Here are some of the walls that you must demolish to enjoy your matrimonial life healthily:

Under the table relationship

Disrespectful demeanor

Resentment

Pretentious attitude

Arrogance
Rebellious conduct
Treacherous conduct
Disloyalty
Untrustworthiness
Premeditate lying
Professional lying
Bad-bred
Infidelity
Dishonesty
Inflexibility
Insincerity
Hypocrisy
Malice
Uncooperative behavior
Hostile behavior
Non-submissiveness
Belligerence
Tenaciousness
Having a loud mouth
Quarrelsomeness
Self-centeredness
Unhealthy conflict-resolution skills
Unhealthy communication skills
Breaching of marriage boundaries
Infringing on matrimonial commitment
Secret relationship with ex boyfriend/ girlfriend or anybody else
Non- total commitment to your spouse.
Non- total acceptance of your spouse
Intolerance
Unhealthy attitude towards your spouse
Unhealthy attitude towards yourself

Untruthfulness
An ungodly character
Ungratefulness
Uncaring attitude
Unappreciative attitude
Unkindness
Spitefulness
Unfaithfulness
Concentrating only on the mistakes of your spouse
Neglecting your spouse physically
Neglecting your spouse emotionally
Neglecting your spouse romantically
Neglecting your spouse intimately
Neglecting your spouse socially
Neglecting your spouse sexually
Neglecting your spouse intellectually
Neglecting your spouse spiritually.

By building walls in your marriage, you are hurting yourself.

Step 17: Total rejection of the under the table relationship pattern.

There are different types of under the table relationships. By the way, what is an under the table relationship? An under the table relationship in marriage is any illicit intimate relationship that you accept to have secretly with another person to please your unhealthy desires of the flesh. It could be with your ex-boyfriend/girlfriend, your boss, your co-worker or anybody else. You choose to do it anyway just to please your feelings, regardless of the outcome and your commitment to be always faithful to your spouse.

Whenever you choose to adopt this behavior, you will lie constantly. If you don't stop practicing it, you could train yourself to be a professional in that matter. Then, you could easily compromise your morality and your core values to satisfy your internal unhealthy secret desires. This is a harmful behavior. In the short term, it might feel good. However, in the long term, it will produce psychological, emotional and spiritual troubles in your own life as well as many other horrible outcomes.

Those who choose to follow the under the table relationship pattern are very bright in that manner. They develop all kinds of strategies to play their spouse and to cover up their secret unhealthy adventure. When they are with their spouse, they act like everything is fine. Some of them are so cunning that they introduce their secret lover to their spouse as a simple friend, a cousin, a classmate, a brother or a sister in the church.

Some of the young people use also the same game to play their parents. The under the table relationship pattern could ruin your life, your marriage and your family. It is a destructive path. Sooner or later, your spouse will definitely discover your dishonesty to your matrimonial vow. Then, you will bring terror and devastation into your entire family. It would be completely wiser to use your skills and your intelligence to keep improving your relationship with your spouse to live honestly, respectfully and faithfully.

Step 18: Keep building bridges in your marriage.

For over a decade, I have traveled by car in several states in the United States of America. For example, from Boston to Huntsville Alabama, I crossed different states and many bridges. The bridges played a key role in my trip. Without them, I would not have been able to get to my destination. If there were walls instead of bridges to separate each state, I would be condemned to travel only in a particular state. It is the same thing in the matrimonial life. If you want to get to your destination in your marriage, you should demolish the walls, and start building bridges.

There is a big difference between a wall and a bridge. A wall and a bridge have two opposite symbolisms. In marriage, the walls symbolize the following elements:

Division
Competition
Insolence
Unhelpfulness
Non-subservience
Lies
Betrayal
Unreliability
Unhealthy communication skills
Bitterness
Irresponsibleness
Non-acceptance
Negligence
Minimizing your spouse
Physical, emotional and psychological abuses
Ingratitude
Poor conflict handling skills
Inadaptability
Hypocrisy
Selfishness
Being full of yourself
Haughtiness
A hate-filled relationship
Uncontrolled temper
Uncontrolled tongue
Being uncommitted
Insularity
Disloyalty

Emotional infidelity

Refusal to listen to your spouse's concern

Refusal to lovingly submit to your spouse

Doing whatever you want

Making decision without first consulting your spouse

Pretending that you are always right

Unaffectionate attitude

Coldness

An undisciplined life

Unhealthy and harmful habits

Treating your spouse in a secondary manner.

I have described some examples of the painful consequences of walls in marriage in chapter three of this book. Let's say that you are married. You choose to keep secretly your relationship with your ex-boyfriend/girlfriend or pretend that it is just a friendly interaction. Your spouse tells you that he or she is not comfortable with that. In spite of his or her concern, you choose to keep your relationship with your so-called friend anyway. This is an example of a big wall that you put up in your own marriage.

Your refusal to pull down this wall could lead in the long term to the destruction of your marriage. Even if your spouse stays quiet for a period of time about it, that doesn't mean that he or she accepts your selfish and destructive behavior. Absolutely, your unwise action will lead to many other problems in your matrimonial life. Finally, it could lead to the devastation of your marriage and your own life. It is always better and wiser to use the preventive method in your marriage and your life in general.

Therefore, I would greatly encourage you to destroy this wall in your marriage. Collaborate lovingly with your spouse to always bring peace and harmony into your matrimonial life. Think about it, your peace of mind is connected with the peace of mind of your spouse. Whenever you choose to take away the peace of mind of your spouse to satisfy your unhealthy desires, you will also lose your own peace of mind.

It is in your own interest and for your own welfare to keep building bridges in your marriage. In marriage the bridges are the symbols of the following points:

Unity
Harmony
Sincerity
Reliability
Vitality
Flexibility
Humility
Loyalty
Cooperation
Affection
Vision
Collaboration
Submission
Sanctification
Healthy communication skills
Healthy conflict resolution skills
Healthy leadership skills
Healthy management skills
Healthy compromises
Healthy habits
Mutual respect
Trustworthiness
Acceptance
Responsibility
Caring
Sound judgment
Adjustment

Commitment

Wisdom

Discipline

Peacemaking

Gratefulness

Treating your spouse with love, respect and dignity

A loving, fun and honest relationship.

Step 19: Do not do to your spouse what you wouldn't accept him or her to do to you.

This principle is very important for the success of your marriage. It is always easier saying certain things than practicing them. Both husband and wife must be willing to practice this principle in their matrimonial life for their own security. This is not the time to play games. This is the time to take seriously your nuptial vow.

Whatever thing you are doing whether secretly or not that could damage your relationship with your spouse, stop it and be honest with God, yourself and your spouse. You may choose to play your partner, but you cannot play God. While you are trying to play your spouse, you are ruining your own life.

Above all else, God is always watching you. You know all the things that you would not accept your spouse to do. Take the same list and apply it in your own life. What you don't want your spouse to do to you, you should not do it to your spouse. There are a lot of things that are very obvious. You don't have to wait for your spouse to tell you not to do it; you should avoid it in the first place. You are responsible for your respect. If you don't respect yourself, who do you think is going to do it for you?

Honesty brings happiness and peace into the matrimonial life. Conversely, dishonesty brings division, shame and painful outcomes in the matrimonial life. In my observation,

I can testify that couples that choose to live in honesty have a better life than those that choose to practice dishonesty. What you choose to practice in your conjugal life is what you will attract in your marital life. God unites you with your spouse to live harmoniously, faithfully and peacefully.

You have one heart. You cannot receive God's blessing in your conjugal life if you choose to keep a secret intimate relationship with your ex-boyfriend/girlfriend or anybody else. It doesn't work like that. In the matrimonial life, fidelity is the path of happiness.

The holy matrimony is a sacred entity. If you choose to keep a secret intimate relationship you will bring disaster and calamity into your own life and your entire family. If you would not tolerate your spouse to do it, you should not do it either. If you want to enjoy healthily your marriage, choose honesty and integrity. Then, you will reap the fruit of joy, peace and happiness.

Step 20: Think, keep thinking and scrutinize healthily your motives, your actions both in public and in secret including your reactions in your matrimonial life.

Do you know who you are? Who are you? I am persuaded that you know who you really are. That's the reason why you know how to introduce yourself as an innocent to get what you want. The same strategy that you have used to present yourself as an angel just to win the heart of your spouse, why don't you apply it in a healthy way in your conjugal life for your own well-being?

So, be truly an angel in your matrimonial life. Of course, you know what you are doing. And also, you know why you choose to do what you are doing in your conjugal life. Absolutely, you are who you are. Yes, who you are is who you are. There is no doubt about it; you will act according to who you are in your marital life, because it is who you are.

You could try to hide who you are during the courtship, the dating and the engagement periods. And, you could be very successful. However, who you are will be revealed as day and night in your matrimonial life. It is not a surprise as it might appear to be; it is exactly who you really are.

Step 21: Self- constructive criticism.

Am I doing my best to create an environment of love, peace, respect and honesty in my conjugal life?

Personal Notes:

Am I a wall builder or a bridge builder in my conjugal life?

Personal Notes:

By God's grace, I want to be and I can be an honest and responsible husband.

Personal Notes:

By God's grace, I want to be and I can be a virtuous wife.

Personal Notes:

By God's grace, I want to and can live honestly and respectfully with my spouse.

Personal Notes:

Step 22: Personal Assessment.

Please, take some time to think and evaluate yourself while you are reading my following thoughts:

Unhappiness in marriage is one of the most internal disturbing pains of mankind.

Evaluate yourself:

A disrespectful, indiscipline, disingenuous, bad-bred and uncontrolled temper woman is like dynamite that is placed under a bridge without supervision that could explode at any moment.

Evaluate yourself:

A disrespectful, indiscipline, disingenuous, bad-bred and uncontrolled tempered man is an insult and a disaster to wisdom, leadership, healthy judgment and humility.

Evaluate yourself:

Marriage is a sacred contract that is based on love, trust, honesty, fidelity and mutual respect. A person who chooses to play the infidelity, disrespect, ruse, manipulation and lie games in his or her marriage, is playing with fire.

Evaluate yourself:

Unfaithfulness and disrespect in matrimonial life are among the major factors that could turn a marriage upside down in a fraction of a second

Evaluate yourself:

An honest Christian woman, who finds an honest Christian man in her conjugal life, should not take the gift of God and the goodness of her husband for granted.

Evaluate yourself:

Blessed is an honest Christian man who finds a virtuous Christian woman.

Evaluate yourself:

Blessed is a virtuous Christian woman who lovingly submits to her husband and nurtures his Christ like leadership with an attitude of respect, reverence and honor to the Almighty King of the Cosmos.

Evaluate yourself:

The matrimonial life of an honest, responsible Christian man and a virtuous Christian woman reflects the unity and the harmony in the Triune God.

Evaluate yourself:

The home of an honest and responsible Christian man and a virtuous Christian woman is a little corner of heaven on planet earth.

Evaluate yourself:

Therefore, I invite you to think and keep thinking about your motives, and your actions both in public and in secret, including your reactions in your matrimonial life.

Evaluate yourself:

Your actions and reactions in your matrimonial life, whether in secret or in public are the visible manifestation of what type of relationship you have with God.

Evaluate yourself:

The way that you choose to live in your matrimonial life shows the level of your seriousness regarding your relationship with your Creator.

Evaluate yourself:

He or she who chooses to have a healthy relationship with God based on honesty, faithfulness, loyalty, integrity, obedience and love will reflect the same behavior in his or her matrimonial life.

Evaluate yourself:

Your commitment to have a healthy marriage:

Your prayer to God:

Chapter 6
Steps To Raise Children

"Train a child in the way he should go, and when he is old he will not turn from it" (Proverbs 22: 6).

With the twenty-first century technology, where many children have access to all kinds of video games, cartoons, cell phones, music, music videos, movies and licentious websites through the Internet, is the sacred duty of parents to raise moral, respectable, responsible and God-fearing children outdated in this age?

A lot of parents all over the world are very busy with their professional life. Contrary to the viewpoint of this world, parents are responsible for forming the character of their children. Each person has his or her own concept of how to raise children.

In spite of the degradation of family values in our society, there are a lot of loving and responsible parents on the four corners of the earth. However, some of them believe that providing abundance of foods and clothes for their children is the accomplishment of their mission as parents.

Others firmly believe that putting many millions of dollars

in a bank account for their children is the main achievement of their parental role. Unfortunately, there are some people who have no problem at all abandoning their children even before their birth. What a tragedy! What a miscalculated decision! What a horrible misstep in life! What a poor judgment with lasting disastrous consequences!

In her book: "Fundamentals of Christian Education", Ellen G. White declared: "Parents need to be impressed with their obligation to give to the world children having well-developed characters, --children who will have moral power to resist temptation, and whose life will be an honor to God and a blessing to their fellow men. Those who enter upon active life with firm principles, will be prepared to stand unsullied amid the moral pollutions of this corrupt age. Let mothers improve every opportunity to educate their children for usefulness.

Parents, you have a work to do for your children which no other can do. You cannot shift your responsibilities upon another. The father's duty to his children cannot be transferred to the mother. If she performs her own duty, she has burden enough to bear. Only by working in unison, can the father and mother accomplish the work which God has committed to their hands."

It is the sacred duty and the responsibility of a father and a mother to raise their children. It is a must. The fruit of the presence, loving care, guidance and the inspirational leadership of a loving and responsible father and mother in the life of a child is priceless and very rewarding in this life and in the life to come. On the other hand, it is a disaster and a human tragedy for some parents to give their demission regarding this divine mandate. The destructive result is none other than the deterioration of our society concerning family values, responsibility, honest citizens, respect and moral principles.

Ellen G White said: "That time is worse than lost to parents and children which is devoted to the acquirement of wealth, while mental improvement and moral culture are neglected. Earthly treasures must pass away; but nobility of character, moral worth, will endure forever. If the work of parents be well done, it will through eternity testify of their wisdom and faithfulness. Those who tax their purses and their ingenuity to the utmost to provide for their households costly apparel and dainty food, or to maintain them in ignorance of useful labor, will be repaid only by the pride, envy, willfulness, and disrespect of their spoiled children.

The young need to have a firm barrier built up from their infancy between them and the world, that its corrupting influence may not affect them. Parents must exercise increasing watchfulness, that their children be not lost to God. If it were considered as important that the young possess a beautiful character and amiable disposition as it is that they imitate the fashions of the world in dress and deportment, we would see hundreds where there is one today coming upon the stage of active life prepared to exert an ennobling influence upon society."

You may ask the question: How do I build up a firm barrier for my children from their childhood between them and the world? Well, let's consult the Book of books which is the Bible. As parents, you are responsible to create a safe environment to raise your children. Here are some of the biblical guidelines:

Teach your children the fear of the Lord from their childhood (Deut 6: 1-9).

Direct your children to keep the way of the Lord and to do what is right and just (Prov 22: 6).

Guide your children to the path of wisdom (Prov. 1: 7).

Discipline your children from their infancy (Prov. 3: 12).

Do not allow your children to follow the path of destruction (Prov 13: 24).

Treat and discipline your children with love and respect (Prov 19: 18).

Teach your children the benefits and the importance of obedience and respect to parents (Exodus 20: 12).

Teach your children discernment and obedience to God's law (Prov 28: 7; Prov 29: 15).

Fathers should not act unreasonably towards their children (Eph 6: 4).

Train your children to be respectful, honest, responsible and to aim high.

Parents must practice what they teach their children.

The husband should protect and treat his wife kindly.

The wife should respect and take care of her husband.

Make your home a center of love, understanding, peace, joy and the application of family values and moral standards.

Parents must spend significant time with their children.

Parents must supervise what kind of video games their children are watching.

Parents must analyze what kind of music their children are listening to.

Parents must keep their children busy with doing something positive.

Parents must read with and for their children.

Parents should go to the library with their children and encourage them to read.

Parents must train their children to memorize some key Bible verses like:

Luke 2: 52; Prov 1: 7; Psalm 119: 9-11; Psalm 119-105; Phi 4: 8; 1 Cor 15: 13; James 1:5; 2 Peter 3: 18; John 3: 16; Isaiah 26: 3; Heb 11: 6; 2 Cor 9: 8; Psalm 100:2; Jeremiah 31:3; Heb 13: 5; John 14:1-3 and many more.

Parents must guide their children regarding the time that they spend watching television.

Parents must develop an extraordinary friendship with their children.

Parents should spend time playing with their children.

Parents must develop a healthy relationship with their children from their childhood.

It is a terrible mistake for parents to set rules for their children without developing a good relationship with them.

Your rules without relationship with your children will push them to the path of disobedience.

Your rules and your loving relationship with your children will guide them to the path of obedience.

Parents must let their children know that they love them and show it through their deeds and words.

Parents have the sacred obligation to train their children to be successful not only in this world, but also and above all in the world to come.

Ellen G. White stated: "The family circle is the school in which the child receives its first and most enduring lessons. Hence parents should be much at home. By precept and example, they should teach their children the love and the fear of God; teach them to be intelligent, social, affectionate, to cultivate habits of industry, economy, and self-denial. By giving their children love, sympathy, and encouragement at home, parents may provide for them a safe and welcome retreat from many of the world's temptations.

No time, "says the father, "I have no time to give to the training of my children, no time for social and domestic enjoyments." Then you should not have taken upon yourself the responsibility of a family. By withholding from them the time which is justly theirs, you rob them of the education which they should have at your hands. If you have children, you have a work to do, in union with the mother, in the formation of their characters.

Those who feel that they have an imperative call to labor for the improvement of society, while their own children grow up undisciplined, should inquire if they have not mistaken their duty. Their own household is the first missionary field in which parents are required to labor. Those who leave the home garden to grow up to thorns and briers, while they manifest great interest in the cultivation of their neighbor's plot of ground, are disregarding the word of God. "

It is completely impossible to have a healthy society by rejecting the family values. Family values have been, were, are and always will be the foundation for preparing responsible and honest citizens in our society. All the great political leaders, religious leaders, achievers, experts and successful people in all generations have received special training in their family of origin. If you had the privilege to ask them, they would tell you that there was a father, a mother, a grandfather, a grandmother, an uncle, an aunt, a big brother, a big sister or a mentor who guided them in the right direction.

Postmodern popular concepts, technology and philosophical speculations cannot replace family values. The deterioration of our society is the direct result of the degradation of family values. The marriage institution is one of the greatest blessings that the Supreme Moral Being of the cosmos has given to the human race to enjoy life happily, responsibly and morally. Family values preserve life, modesty, morality, decency, civility, moderation; they prepare respectful, responsible and honest citizens for this world and the world to come.

I greatly applaud the following affirmations of Ellen G. White: "Society is composed of families, and is what the heads of families make it. Out of the heart are "the issues of life"; and the heart of the community, of the church, and of the nation is the household. The well-being of society, the success of the church, the prosperity of the nation, depend upon home influences.

The elevation or deterioration of the future of society will be determined by the manners and morals of the youth growing up around us. As the youth are educated, and as their characters are molded in their childhood to virtuous habits, self-control, and temperance, so will their influence be upon society. If they are left unenlightened and uncontrolled, and as a result become self-willed, intemperate in appetite and passion, so will be their future influence in molding society. The company which the young now keep, the habits they now form, and the principles they now adopt are the index to the state of society for years to come.

The home that is beautified by love, sympathy, and tenderness is a place that angels love to visit, and where God is glorified. The influence of a carefully guarded Christian home in the years of childhood and youth is the surest safeguard against the corruptions of the world. In the atmosphere of such a home the children will learn to love both their earthly parents and their heavenly Father."

Parents are responsible for forming the character of their children from their childhood. According to the pattern of this world, it appears that money is the greatest heritage of parents to their children. There is nothing wrong in having a lot of money. We all need and use money. There is no doubt about it, money could bring to your children fame, popularity, power and many more privileges in this world.

However, money cannot and will never be able to form the character of your children. Therefore, the greatest heritage of parents to their children is to form their character from their childhood and prepare them to be successful, respectful and responsible citizens for this world and the world to come.

Addressing the fundamental role of parents, Ellen G. White asserted: "The work of the mother is sacred and important. She should teach her children, from the cradle up, habits of self-denial and self-control. Her time, in a special sense, belongs to her children. But if it is mostly occupied with the follies of this degenerate age, if society, dress, and amusements absorb her attention, her children will fail to be suitably educated.

Would that the mothers of this generation might feel the sacredness of their mission, not trying to vie with their wealthy neighbors in appearance, but seeking to honor God by the faithful performance of duty. If right principles in regard to temperance were implanted in the youth who are to form and mold society, there would be little necessity for temperance crusades. Firmness of character, moral control, would prevail, and in the strength of Jesus the temptations of these last days would be resisted.

A sacred trust is committed to parents, to guard the physical and moral constitutions of their children, so that the nervous system may be well balanced, and the soul not endangered. Fathers and mothers should understand the laws of life, that they may not, through ignorance, allow wrong tendencies to develop in their children."

There are troublemakers, ill-balanced minds, injudicious tempers, disrespectful and undisciplined people in both the secular and the religious world. Their behaviors have a lot to do with the environment they grew up in. Their actions are greatly related to the failure of their parents to discipline them from their childhood.

Ellen G. White declared: "Fathers and mothers should carefully and prayerfully study the characters of their children. They should seek to repress and restrain those traits that are too prominent, and to encourage others which may be deficient, thus securing harmonious development. This is no light matter. The father may not consider it a great sin to neglect the training of his children; but thus does God regard it. Christian parents need a thorough conversion upon this subject. Guilt is accumulating upon them, and the consequences of their actions reach down from their own children to children's children. The ill-balanced mind, the hasty temper, the fretfulness, envy, or jealousy, bear witness to parental neglect. These evil traits of character bring great unhappiness to their possessors. How many fail to receive from companions and friends the love, which they might have, if they were more amiable. How many create trouble wherever they go, and in whatever they are engaged!"

There is no bright future without family values and standards. The "prince of this world" who is Satan knows that very well. That's the reason why he establishes all kinds of distractions on the four corners of the earth to minimize the sacred duty and the importance of family. Any attack on family is an attack against the future of our society and our civilization. Man did not establish the foundation of family.

The Supreme Moral Monarch of the cosmos establishes the foundation of family. The concepts of this world about family values are contrary to God's ordinances. Believe it or not, practice it or not, what a child learns at home greatly affect our interactions as human beings. Parents should do their best to accomplish their mission faithfully.

According to Ellen G. White: "A sacred duty rests upon parents to guide their children into paths of strict obedience. True happiness in this life and in the future life depends upon obedience to a "Thus saith the Lord." Parents, let Christ's life be the pattern. Satan will devise every possible means to break down this high standard of piety as one altogether too strict. It is your work to impress upon your children in their early years the thought that they are formed in the image of God. Christ came to this world to give them a living example of what they all must be, and parents who claim to believe the truth for this time are to teach their children to love God and to obey His law. This is the greatest and most important work that fathers and mothers can do. . . . It is God's design that even the children and youth shall understand intelligently what God requires, that they may distinguish between righteousness and sin, between obedience and disobedience."

In this age, some parents neglect their duty as the first teachers of their children. Unfortunately, some of them let the entertainment industries play their sacred role in the lives of their children. When I was growing up, my father and my mother were my first teachers in everything. They taught me a lot of good things that I didn't study in school. I am very grateful to them. The guidance of my parents from my childhood helps me to face life in general in a healthy way.

Ellen White declared: "The father and the mother should be the first teachers of their children. Fathers and mothers need to understand their responsibility. The world is full of snares for the feet of the young. Multitudes are attracted by a life of selfish and sensual pleasure. They cannot discern the hidden dangers or the fearful ending of the path that seems to them the way of happiness. Through the indulgence of appetite and passion, their energies are wasted, and millions are ruined for this world and for the world to come. Parents should remember that their children must encounter these temptations. Even before the birth of the child, the preparation should begin that will enable it to fight successfully the battle against evil. "

It was at the feet of my parents that I learned from my childhood the basic principles of life such as: wisdom, discipline, self-control, honesty, loyalty, morality, humility, trustworthiness, healthy thinking and conviction to follow the right path of life. They taught me to always rely on God, to be obedient, to be responsible, to be respectful, to be kind, to be content, to serve, to help and to always treat others with respect and dignity.

Ellen G. White stated: "Parents should educate their children line upon line, precept upon precept, here a little and there a little, not allowing any disregard of God's holy law. They should rely upon divine power, asking the Lord to help them to keep their children true to Him who gave His only-begotten Son to bring the disloyal and disobedient back to their allegiance. God longs to pour upon men and women the rich current of His love. He longs to see them delighting to do His will, using every jot of their entrusted powers in His service, teaching all who come within the sphere of their influence that the way to be treated as righteous for Christ's sake is to obey the law."

There are a lot of loving, responsible and wonderful parents all over the world. Personally, I praise God for my parents. I still remember my wonderful childhood experiences with my parents. My father was my hero, my mentor and my coach. He helped me develop my intellectual curiosity from an early age. I still remember how he used to play with me and guide me in the right path. My affectionate mother was wonderful. After Jesus Christ, her guidance from my babyhood transforms my life. I have such an excellent souvenir of my mother because she practiced what she taught me. A few weeks before the death of my mother, I wrote and described her name to express my thanks to her. The name of my mother was Rose Charles. Here is what I wrote on her behalf before her death:

Respectable and loving mother, I thank you.

On your loving and tender care, I grew up.

Sound, you do form my character, I love you.

Excitedly, your guidance, I follow up.

Christ likely, you always treat other people.

Heavenly heritage is your main reward.

Affection is real in you, model couple.

Rejoice, God will always bless your vineyard.

Lord, please, let your light shine on my mother.

Elation, peace and eternal joy to you

Servant of the Almighty God, thank you, mother.

My kindhearted mother was a woman of noble character.

She was a scrupulous woman.

She was a moral woman.

She was a woman of faith.

She was a respectful woman.

She was a virtuous woman.

She was a faithful and honest wife.

She was a trustworthy wife.

She was a respectful wife

She was a responsible wife.

She was a loyal wife.

She was a reliable wife.

She was a wonderful mother.

She was a blessed mother.

Above all, she was a true servant of the Most High King of the universe.

It is a blessing to be raised by a mother of noble character.

Chapter 7
Romance In Marriage

"Your lips are like a strand of scarlet,

And your mouth is lovely.

Your temples behind your veil

Are like a piece of pomegranate.

Your neck is like the tower of David,

Built for an armory,

On which hang a thousand bucklers,

All shields of mighty men." (Song of Songs 4: 3-4)

A few years ago, I was invited to help a couple to deal with some family issues. The wife was a nurse. She knew a lot of things about the human anatomy. The husband was less educated in that matter. However, the husband firmly believed that he should be the one to teach his wife everything. He refuses to pay attention to his wife's concern regarding romance in their marriage.

According to the wife testimony, she tried many times to explain to her husband that there are differences between a man and a woman. Therefore, there is a certain way that a husband should approach his wife. Instead of letting his wife expresses herself, he always accuses her of cheating. His reaction was:" How do you know all these things? I am your husband. I'm supposed to show you everything about sexuality." The wife was completely frustrated.

During the meeting, the wife said:" He comes and gives me two children. That's all. He never takes time for cuddling, caressing and kissing." What is your mental image of your marriage? Do you have a vision for your marriage? Do you know where you are in your marriage lifetime's journey? Do you know where you want to be? How is the vitality of your marriage?

Romance is very significant in marriage. To enjoy your matrimonial life healthily, it is a must to keep the flame of your family worship altar burning. As you properly maintain the flame of your family worship altar burning, you must also keep the flame of romance burning in your marriage.

Negligence, irresponsibility, carelessness and erroneous conception of spirituality in that matter could have disastrous consequences. A lot of people do not pay enough attention to romance in their conjugal life. Romance in marriage covers a variety of things. Believe it or not, whether you notice it or not, the vitality of your marriage has a lot to do with romance.

There are some people who pretend that they are so spiritual, they don't have time for romance. Therefore, they don't have any problem neglecting their spouse romantically. When their spouse starts to complain about it, they always find something to justify themselves.

Some of them pretend that they are busy in the proclamation of the gospel. Others claim that they are completely busy with their occupation. They go further to say that their profession is very demanding. So, there is nothing that they can do about it. In spite of all the good arguments, excuses cannot and would not solve this urgent problem in the matrimonial life.

How many wives are suffering on that matter all over the world? Some of them are suffering silently. Others find their own way to fill this empty space in their lives. There are a lot of little things that may appear insignificant; however, they constitute the tools to enjoy your marriage happily.

It doesn't matter what your occupation is; you should do your best to keep the flame of romance burning in your matrimonial life. There are a lot of things that you could do to keep your marriage alive romantically. Here are some helpful tips:

1. Make yourself comfortable to tell your spouse: I love you.

May be, you might say this is the simplest thing to say in matrimonial life. However, for some people, it is completely different. You may not think about it, there are a lot of people in some places in the world who do not follow this practice. According to their culture, they express their love to their partner silently or in writing. That's the way they choose to convey their love for their wives. It is good to articulate your love for your spouse in writing.

However, it is very important to also express your love verbally to your spouse. When you constantly say to your spouse that you love him or her verbally, there is something deeper that is going on in your relationship. If you want to know the importance of this approach in your marital life, discuss it with your wife. I am persuaded that she will tell you how she feels about it and what impact it has on her.

Therefore, I encourage you to make it a habit in your conjugal life to intermittently say to your spouse: I love you. It means a lot more than what you think or imagine. It should be a continuous process. If you practice this method, surely, you will eat its delicious fruit. Your wife will become more and more sweet. She will develop a loving smile that you have never seen before on her face.

There is no doubt about it, your wife wants you from time to time to remind her verbally how much you love her. She doesn't want it to be a secret. She wants to hear it from you. By the way, she is always ready to hear it from you. She will never be tired of hearing from you. On the contrary, when you take a break in that matter, she will tell you: "Nowadays, you don't tell me anymore that you love me". This is her way of notifying you that she wants you to continuously tell her that you love her.

2. Never stop dating your spouse.

Do you remember the excitement when you were on the verge of winning the heart of your spouse? At that time, you were ready to make any sacrifice to achieve your goal. Use your imagination and creativity to develop more dating skills than ever before to enjoy life romantically with your spouse.

3. Make plans to take your spouse out from time to time.

There are a lot of beautiful places all over the world that you could go with your spouse. You could take your partner on a cruise. Of course, it depends on your possibilities. Effectively, you should act according to your possibilities. However, you don't have to wait until you have a lot of money to put into practice this method.

You could take your spouse to one of the best restaurants in your community. You could go to the museum together. You could take your spouse to the beach. You could invite your spouse to enjoy a presentation from your local Symphony Orchestra. You could go to the park with your spouse. You could spend a weekend with your spouse in one of the best hotels in your area. There are a lot of things that you could do.

4. Make decent jokes together.

Do not make of your marriage a burden. Marriage is wonderful. There is fun in marriage. Therefore, play together with your spouse. Laugh together with your spouse. Make jokes together with your spouse. Be comfortable with discussing any topic together. Express yourself freely. Communicate with each other respectfully about what you like and what you don't like in everything including intimacy and sexuality.

Relax, be creative and play some games together. There are some husbands who are fooling themselves by pretending that they are so spiritual, they don't have time to have fan with their wives. I encourage you to do your best to avoid this type of mistake in your matrimonial life.

5. Remember the important dates.

When I was dating my wife, I went to a store to buy a gift for her birthday. The lady who was wrapping the gift said: "Do you buy this beautiful gift for your wife?" I replied: "no, I'm buying it for my girlfriend". She asserted: "Oh! You're buying it for your girlfriend? Since our marriage, my husband never buys me anything. He doesn't even remember my birthday." It was hearth breaking for her. Some people do not realize it or do not pay attention in that matter. However, birthdays, anniversaries, Valentine's Day, and marriage anniversaries mean a lot to your wife. She is watching your reaction towards these dates.

There are a lot of things that you could do to celebrate these significant dates. Both husband and wife should remember them and show their appreciation for each other. You don't need to spend a lot of money. A card, a poem and any small gift would make your wife happy for her birthday. In your matrimonial life, do not let these dates pass without showing your love, your appreciation and your commitment to spend the rest of your life in the arms of your spouse.

6. Make it a habit to hug your spouse and hold hands together.

When you wake up in the morning, after your devotional prayer, give a hug and a good day kiss to your spouse before heading to work. When you come back from work or a trip, hug and kiss your partner to show how happy you are to be home together. At night, after the family worship, give a hug and a loving good night kiss to your partner. When you are walking with your spouse, hold hands together. There is magnetism in this approach that will greatly increase your emotional bond.

7. Make it a habit to buy flowers, gifts and loving cards for your spouse.

You don't have to wait for a special occasion to buy a flower, a gift or a card for your wife. You could do it any time you think that it is necessary to do so. It is good, romantic and fun to surprise your wife in that matter. For example, you could send flowers to your wife at her job without notifying her. You could leave a love note or a card for your spouse in the house. From time to time, you could surprise your spouse with a loving phone call.

8. Sexual Intimacy

In the beginning of this chapter, I have mentioned a lady who was complaining about the approach of her husband regarding sexual intimacy. She was frustrated because her husband did not follow the basic steps of sexual intimacy. If you want to be a lawyer, you don't just go and practice law. There is a period of preparation that you must follow to practice your profession. It is the same thing for sexual intimacy.

Sexual intimacy has several phases. Before reaching the peak of sexual intimacy efficiently, one must first follow the different preparatory stages. When you have the desire to travel in the universe of your wife, you must notify her of your intention, and always climb her ladder step by step. There is no need to rush. You don't have to rush. Naturally, she doesn't function like that. Therefore, take your time to efficiently explore the different avenues of the universe of your wife until you reach your main destination.

Here are some of the preliminary stages:

Loving look.

Loving talk.

Articulate your admiration for your wife.

Hugging

Holding tight

Holding closer and closer

Embracing

Caressing

Kissing

Loving small touch

Loving massage

Cuddling

Smooching

Snuggling

Necking

Keep reiterating your love and your commitment to your spouse by your words and your actions.

Through your actions and your words, make the following components a reality in your conjugal life:

Flexibility.

Admiration.

Adaptability.

Mutual respect.

Spirituality.

Reliability.

Loyalty and kindness.

Tolerance.

Fidelity.

Unselfishness.

Willingness to listen to each other.

Understanding.

Non-hypocritical acceptance.

Empathy

Recognize, respect and accept your differences.

Mutual dedication.

Resolving conflict constructively.

Taking joy in each other's accomplishments.

Let the communication lines be always wide open.

Communicate with respect and decency.

Always spend significant time together.

Willingness to forgive each other.

Do not cultivate rancor against your spouse.

Demonstrate your affection through your words and your deeds.

Never cease praying together and for each other.

Enjoy life at its highest level with your spouse.

To enjoy the matrimonial life healthily in its totality, both husband and wife must have the mental disposition to stay together until death by living:

Faithfully

Honestly

Physically

Socially

Emotionally

Spiritually

Intellectually

Kindly
Joyfully
Tenderly
Respectfully
Happily
Gently
Amiably
Cordially
Affably
Pleasantly
Devotedly
Cheerily
Confidentially
Delightfully
Closely
Amusingly
Blissfully
Ecstatically
Adoringly
Lovingly
Amorously
Affectionately
Romantically
Charmingly
Intimately
Sexually.

Chapter 8
Dimensions of Marriage

A godly character, responsible, respectful, well-bred and honest Christian man who finds a loving, honest, responsible, respectful, well-bred and godly character Christian woman in his matrimonial life, is one step closer to eternal life.

Martial A. Charles

We are approaching the end of our wonderful journey on marriage. We have been traveling from the first week of the creation of planet earth to our century. In the final stop on our trip, we are going to talk about the two fundamental dimensions of marriage. I am convinced that this topic has a vital significance that we should take into consideration for our own eternal happiness. A lot of children all over the world are very confused, as never before, about marriage in the Twenty-First Century.

In this technological age where the media in its various forms, including the social networks are spreading all kinds of information about the lifestyles of a lot of people around the world and their own concepts about the institution of marriage, it is easy for many children to be confused about the sanctity of marriage. Not only the children, there are also many adults on the face of the earth who are confused.

Some of them even reject their previous beliefs in order to conform themselves to the current inclinations of this age regarding marriage. The popular tendencies, arguments and various opinions concerning marriage in our century are contrary to the Word of God. The rejection of the sanctity of marriage by our society is one of the most visible signs that we are living at the last stage of the history of this world. In this chapter, you will discover that man can only find true success and true happiness in marriage and life in general in God.

You don't have to be a scholar to understand that sumptuous lifestyles, material wealth and the shaky emotional and psychological stability that some people are enjoying in this world are not really the pinnacle of true success and happiness on all levels of life. In spite of all these things, we are unable to reach the mountaintop of true happiness by ourselves. Everything that we possess comes from God. Our five senses derive from God our Creator.

Therefore, everything that we can see, hear, smell, taste and touch is the direct act of the Maker of heaven and earth. Looking for true happiness away from God is the path of self-deception. A simple look at the two fundamental dimensions of marriage will help us to see evidently both the physical and the spiritual realities of eternal happiness.

Marriage has two fundamental dimensions. The first one is the physical dimension. The second one is the spiritual dimension. To help you grasp the vital essence of the two fundamental dimensions of marriage, I am going to take a tour with you on the first week of the creation of planet earth. God is the Absolute Spiritual and Moral Being in both and beyond the visible and the invisible world. In His invisibility, the Immortal King of the cosmos called the visible world into existence.

Therefore, the visible world exists through invisible means that only the Almighty Ruler of the outer space can see, understand, explain and control. The Supreme Monarch of the visible and the invisible world has neither beginning nor end. In His invisibility, the Supreme Designer of the cosmos can make the invisible visible as He wishes.

However, everything else both in the visible and the invisible world has a beginning. In His infinite, invisible and incomprehensible Power, the Maker of heaven and earth laid the foundation of the visible and the invisible world. Only by speaking, the Creator of the visible and the invisible world brought all things into existence (Ps 33; 6, 9; 148:5; Heb 11: 3).

In His first creative Word to call into existence the visible world, the One true God called forth light to shine upon the earth (Genesis 1:3). It was not a matter of chance. It was not an accident. It was not a coincidence. It was not a cosmic explosion. The light didn't appear by itself. It was the direct result of the majestic act of the Creator of the universe.

Deductively, it was a well-calculated providential act. Before this divine activity, the earth didn't have a form. It was empty. And, there was darkness on the earth (Genesis1: 1-2). By scrutinizing Genesis 1: 1-2 deeply, under the influence of the Holy Spirit, we can firmly conclude that life was not possible on earth prior to the six days of creative activity of the Almighty God.

In His invisibility, inconceivable and immeasurable power, the Supreme Majesty of the visible and the invisible world calls light into existence on planet earth for two fundamental purposes. Before going further, let me try to give you a simple idea of the infinite greatness of our Creator. God, in His invisibility, the invisible is visible. God is the Supreme Mystery. In His mystery, there is no mystery for Him. Therefore, there is no invisible for God in His invisibility. So, the Maker of heavens and earth is the Invisible Himself. This is the mystery of the invisibility of the Supreme Monarch of the universe.

Here are some aspects of God's realm:

Indiscernible

Invisible

Incomprehensible

Imperceptible

Inexplicable

Interminable

Inestimable

Immeasurable

Indescribable

Inconceivable

Impenetrable

Unimaginable

Unthinkable

Undetectable

Unnoticeable

Unremarkable

Untraceable

Unrestricted

Unbounded

Uninterrupted

Unexplained

Undisclosed

Unlimited

Uncontrolled

Unrestrained

Unconstrained

Unrevealed

Endless

Countless

Boundless

Ceaseless

Infinite

Mysterious

Unseen

Eternal

God reveals Himself to mankind. What we know about and of God comes not from our intellect, creativity or imagination; but from God's own revelation. The Invisible and Immortal King of heavens and earth decided to make His creative works visible and life possible on planet earth. These are the two fundamental purposes that He said:" Let there be light, and there was light"(Genesis 1: 3).

Before that statement from the Supreme Monarch of the cosmos, the earth was covered with physical darkness. Life was not possible. By speaking, God brings light and makes life possible on earth. On the sixth day of His creative activity, God created man in "His image and likeness (Genesis 1:26-27). "And the LORD God formed man of the dust of the ground, and breathed into his nostrils the breath of life; and man became a living being" (Genesis 2: 7).

As we have discussed in the first chapter, God established the institution of marriage. He gave Eve to Adam. God celebrated Adam's wedding on the sixth day of creation week. And, on the seventh day of His creative activity, "God rested, blessed and sanctified the seventh day"(Genesis 2: 1-3).

As mentioned in the first chapter, the first wedding on planet earth was between Adam and Eve. Adam was the groom, and Eve was the bride. Adam and Eve received the divine benediction. Literally, God gave Eve to Adam as his sweetie for life. Adam and Eve were united in holy matrimony to enjoy life together harmoniously in all aspects. This is the physical dimension of marriage.

In the physical dimension, a man and a woman united together literally, publicly and visibly in the holy matrimony to live officially as husband and wife. In the physical dimension, both husband and wife have the responsibility and the sacred duty to nurture their matrimonial life, produce fruit with their gift of procreation and take care of their children. Absolutely, both husband and wife are responsible for making their marriage a success.

The physical dimension of marriage does not mean that marriage is exclusively a natural thing. On the contrary, the physical dimension of marriage is the visible manifestation of God's relationship with the human race. God is not only the Author of life. He is also the Author of marriage. God determines the principles that govern marriage. He created man with the need of a companion. He defines the role of the husband and the role of the wife. Marriage is sacred both in the physical and the spiritual dimensions. No creature both in the natural and the supernatural realms can modify the sacred character of marriage.

Here are some of the fundamental characteristics of marriage:

Divine in origin

Sacred

Companionship

Unbreakable union between a man and a woman

Monogamous

Heterosexual

Transcend human choices, opinions and regulations.

In the physical dimension of marriage, the Maker of heaven and earth establishes the rules, the roles and the responsibilities for the family unit. Obedience to God's plan brings joy, peace, harmony and happiness. Conversely, disobedience to God's plan produces misery, division, disrespect, disaster, disappointment, pain, shame, guilt, animosity, humiliation, sorrow, despair, unhappiness and many other disastrous consequences.

If you are not convinced of this affirmation, take a look in our postmodern society. What do you see? Are family values the nucleus of our society? What are the consequences of the rejection of family and marriage principles?

Family is the foundation of human society. When men choose to reject the vital and moral principles that govern family, they turn society upside down. It is completely impossible to have a stable society by destroying the fundamental building blocks of human society.

Here are some of the consequences of the rejection of family and marriage principles:

Sexual promiscuity

Promotion of immorality

Promotion of infidelity

Promotion of uncontrolled sexual activities

Promotion of pre-marital sex

Promotion of the disintegration of marriage and family

Promotion of cohabitation

Perversion

Abomination

Self-gratification

Confusion

Licentious lifestyles

Single parents homes

Juvenile delinquency

Teenage pregnancy

Degradation of society

Degradation of human lucidity

Despair

Social upheaval

Injustice

Dysfunctional families

Promotion of divorce

Disaster

Hatred

Self-indulgence

Self-delusion

Self-destruction

Self-glorification

Self-deception

Rejection of monogamous marriage

Rejection of responsibility

Rejection of family values

Rejection of crucial principles of family

Rejection of disciplinary measures

Rejection of self-discipline

Rejection of heterosexual relationship

Rejection of genuine commitment

Rejection of the moral basis of human society

Rejection of the moral standards of human civilization

Rejection of the Moral Law of God.

The movement for the deterioration of marriage and family in our century has a cosmic antecedent. The popular campaign in our era to demolish the institution of marriage is not as simple a thing as it may appear. Definitely, it is a fundamental element of the great controversy between Jesus Christ and Satan. **

The goal of Satan, who is the master deceiver of the human race, is to destroy God's image in man. His first evil strike on the human race was in the Garden of Eden. Unfortunately, Eve decided to obey him instead of God. And, you know the horrible consequences of Eve's choice. Before the final destruction of this sinful world, Satan is preparing two final evil strikes to turn the human race away from God. The first one is on the marriage institution. The second one is on the Sabbath.

Satan is not a friend of the human race. On the contrary, he is the worst enemy of the human race. Therefore, the official rejection of the marriage institution and the official rejection of the Sabbath in the last days of the history of this world as clearly stated in the Bible from Genesis to Revelation by the human race will be the most solemn signs that we are on the final stage of the destruction of this world.

So, the erroneous viewpoint of marriage in our era is not an accident. Believe it or not, the campaign against the sanctity of marriage in the last days of the history of this world is one of the greatest harms to humanity. As we have explained in the first chapter of this book, the marriage institution and the Seventh-day Sabbath are the two indestructible institutions that the Creator of the universe had established before the entrance of sin on planet earth. Any attack against these two unbreakable institutions is a direct attack against the Supreme Ruler of the cosmos.

Therefore, the official rejection of these two institutions by mankind will finally lead to the destruction of this world. In the last days of the history of this shaky world, there will be more and more an aggressive worldwide official campaign against the sanctity of marriage and of the Seventh-day Sabbath as the day of rest. The campaign against the Sabbath as the day of rest will be totally worse than the campaign against the sanctity of marriage. If you want to know more about the horrible events of the last days of this world, please, read my book: The Imminence Of The New World.

The sanctity of marriage is for the well-being of the human race. The union of a man and a woman in holy matrimony is God's plan for the happiness of mankind both in the physical and the spiritual dimensions. Any deviation in that matter is against the plan of God. It will definitely produce hefty consequences.

Absolutely, the breakdown of marriage and families has a cosmic connection.

Absolutely, the disintegration of marriage and families is an attack against God.

Absolutely, the degeneration of marriage and families is a failure of mankind.

Absolutely, the crumbling of marriage and families is a disaster to humanity.

Absolutely, the collapse of marriage and families is a dire blow to human beings.

Absolutely, the dissolution of marriage and families is a tragedy to mankind.

Absolutely, the deterioration of marriage and families is an insult to humanity.

Absolutely, the relapse of marriage and families is a slur to human civilization.

Absolutely, the falling apart of marriage and families is a horrible thing.

Absolutely, the reversion of marriage and families is a human devastation.

Absolutely, the disbanding of marriage and families is a human calamity.

Absolutely, the annihilation of marriage and families will produce harsh fruits.

Absolutely, the destabilization of marriage and families in the last days of the history of mankind is a part of the great controversy between Jesus Christ and Satan.

The physical dimension of marriage is the visible reflection of the spiritual dimension of marriage. The physical dimension of marriage comes into existence through the spiritual dimension of marriage. Therefore, the physical dimension of marriage cannot be productive without connecting to the spiritual dimension of marriage. Apart from the spiritual dimension of marriage, the physical dimension of marriage cannot survive by itself. God created man in "His image and likeness." Consequently, man was born in the physical dimension with a total spiritual connection with the Creator of the universe.

So, God was the Author of life and the Provider for Adam in both the spiritual and the physical dimensions of marriage. When God gave Eve to Adam as his helper, Adam was condemned to develop with Eve in the physical dimension the same relationship that he has with Him in the spiritual dimension. God trained Adam to obey Him lovingly and voluntarily both in the physical and the spiritual dimensions. God trained Eve to submit herself to her husband Adam in the physical dimension as she was trained to obey God lovingly and voluntarily in the spiritual dimension.

This is the only way to have a healthy marriage in the following levels:

Physically

Emotionally

Psychologically

Socially

Respectfully

Honestly

Faithfully

Sincerely

Intimately

Romantically

Mentally

Lovingly

Spiritually

Sexually

Now, we are going to briefly describe biblically the spiritual dimension of marriage. Even if we are living in a sinful world, the divine order to have a healthy marriage remains the same. We witness and clearly see the unpleasant and horrific consequences of the violation of God's order regarding husband and wife from Eve's disobedience to the divine order of marriage to our time.

Humankind cannot live happy and in peace without God. Loving obedience to God is the way of true peace both in the physical and the spiritual dimensions. Therefore, not only in the natural realm, but also in the supernatural realm, no creature can live in peace without the Almighty King of the universe. God is the Supreme Provider both in the physical and the spiritual dimensions. Consequently, the human race must turn to God to enjoy inner peace and to live truly happy.

Spiritually, Adam and Eve were born united with God. God gave them the possibility to enjoy together the same union in the physical dimension. It is a lifetime commitment both in the physical and the spiritual dimensions. Unfortunately, Eve decided to follow her own feelings instead of obeying God's vital principles. That's the reason why there is so much confusion in the world specifically about God and the sanctity of marriage.

The good news is our loving heavenly Father has prepared a wonderful rescue plan for the human race. Through this loving act of God, the original plan of God for humankind is still active. All those who accept Jesus as their Savior and Lord will have the privilege of participating in the greatest nuptial ceremony in all eternity. That's why the prophet Isaiah declared:

"For your Maker is your husband,

The LORD of hosts is His name;

And your Redeemer is the Holy One of Israel;

He is called the God of the whole earth" (Isaiah 54: 5)

The Bible depicts Jesus Christ as the groom and the church as the bride (Mat 9:15; Jn 3: 29; 1 Co 6: 15; Rev 19: 7-9; 21: 2). The church is not a building. The church is composed of all the faithful followers of Christ of all generations from Adam to the glorious second coming of Christ. The Source of life stated:

"I will betroth you to Me forever;

Yes, I will betroth you to Me in righteousness and in justice,

In loving kindness and in compassion,

And I will betroth you to Me in faithfulness.

Then you will know the LORD" (Hosea 2: 19-20).

At the end of the history of this world, the bride will be officially married to the groom. The church will be married to Jesus Christ (Rev 19: 6-8; Rev 21: 2; 9-11). Are you ready to meet Jesus? Is it your choice to marry Him forever? He is coming soon. Do you plan to be a part of the most wonderful nuptial ceremony in all eternity? Adam will be there. Noah will be there. Abraham will be there. Moses will be there. Esther will be there. The apostles Peter, Paul and John will be there. By God's grace and through the guidance of the Holy Spirit, I plan to be there. Do you plan to be there? Will you be there?

What do you do with the universal loving appeal of our Lord and Savior Jesus Christ who died on Calvary for your sins?

There is no mystery about it. It is not for a particular nation.

There is no mystery about it. It is not for a particular tribe.

There is no mystery about it. It is not for a particular country.

There is no mystery about it. It is not for a particular class in our society.

There is no mystery about it. It is not for a particular group of people.

There is no mystery about it. It is for all the inhabitants of the earth.

There is no mystery about it. It doesn't matter what is your ideology.

There is no mystery about it. It doesn't matter what is your own system of beliefs.

There is no mystery about it. It doesn't matter what is your philosophical approach.

There is no mystery about it. It doesn't matter what is your creed.

There is no mystery about it. It doesn't matter what is your article of faith.

There is no mystery about it. It doesn't matter what is your profession of faith.

There is no mystery about it. It doesn't matter how you choose to live.

There is no mystery about it. It doesn't matter what is your own concepts regarding the Creator of the universe.

There is no mystery about it. It doesn't matter what is your own perception of life.

There is no mystery about it. It doesn't matter what is your way of life.

There is no mystery about it. It doesn't matter what is your own opinion about God.

There is no mystery about it. This appeal is for the human race in its totality.

There is no mystery about it. Whether you acknowledge it or not, this appeal irrevocably concerns all the human beings on planet earth.

Therefore, " Come and drink freely The Water of Life."

Come and drink freely The Water of Life, the super rich people of this world.

Come and drink freely The Water of Life, the rich people of this world.

Come and drink freely The Water of Life, the super middle class people of this world.

Come and drink freely The Water of Life, the middle class people of this world.

Come and drink freely The Water of Life, the poor people of this world.

Come and drink freely The Water of Life, the celebrities of this world.

Come and drink freely The Water of Life, the leaders of this world

Come and drink freely The Water of Life, the experts of this world

Come and drink freely The Water of Life, the famous people of this world.

Come and drink freely The Water of Life, the oppressed people of this world.

Come and drink freely The Water of Life, the rejected people of this world.

Come and drink freely The Water of Life, the humiliated people of this world.

Come and drink freely The Water of Life, the persecuted people in this world.

Come and drink freely The Water of Life, the outcasts of this world.

Come and drink freely The Water of Life, the homeless of this world

Come and drink freely The Water of Life, those who are starving in this world.

Come and drink freely The Water of Life, those who are living in poverty in this world.

Come and drink freely The Water of Life, those who do not have access to clean water in this world.

Come and drink freely The Water of Life, the healthy people of this word.

Come and drink freely The Water of Life, the unhealthy people of this world.

Come and drink freely The Water of Life, the fortunate people of this world.

Come and drink freely The Water of Life, the unfortunate people of this world.

Come and drink freely The Water of Life, the scholars of this world.

Come and drink freely The Water of Life, the uneducated people of this world.

Come and drink freely The Water of Life, the wise of this world.

Come and drink freely The Water of Life, the fools of this world.

Come and drink freely The Water of Life, the great men and women of this world.

Come and drink freely The Water of Life, the pariahs of this world.

Come and drink freely The Water of Life, the Nobility of this world.

Come and drink freely The Water of Life, the people of this world.

Come and drink freely The Water of Life, the first class citizens of this world.

Come and drink freely The Water of Life, the second- class citizens of this world.

Come and drink freely The Water of Life, the third class citizens of this world.

Come and drink freely The Water of Life, the kings, queens and emperors of this world.

Come and drink freely The Water of Life, the housekeepers of this world.

Come and drink freely The Water of Life, the billionaires of this world.

Your personal decision to give the control of your mind, your heart and your will to Jesus Christ:

Bibliography of Works Cited

White, Ellen G. Adventist Home. Hagerstown, MD: Review and Herald Publishing Association, 1980.

White, Ellen G. Child Guidance. Washington, D.C.: Review and Herald Publishing Association, 1954.

White, Ellen G. Fundamentals of Christian Education. Nashville, TN: Southern Publishing Association, 1923.

Would you like to see your manuscript become a book?

If you are interested in becoming a PublishAmerica author, please submit your manuscript for possible publication to us at:

acquisitions@publishamerica.com

You may also mail in your manuscript to:

**PublishAmerica
PO Box 151
Frederick, MD 21705**

www.publishamerica.com